COGAN'S
WOODS

MARCH 1ST

For Carolyn,
    Who always treated
me well and looked after
me at NKU! I know
Fred and Rainwater would
like this story! Hope to
see you soon!   BEST,
                Rm

COGAN'S WOODS

RON ELLIS

PRUETT
PUBLISHING
BOULDER, COLORADO

2001

Printed in the United States of America

10 09 08 07 06 05 04 03 02 01   5 4 3 2 1

Library of Congress Cataloging-in-Publication Data

Ellis, Ron, 1949–
   Cogan's Woods / Ron Ellis.
       p. cm.
   ISBN 0-87108-915-7 (alk. paper)
     1. Fathers and sons—Fiction. 2. Squirrel hunting—Fiction.
   3. Outdoor life—Fiction. 4. Kentucky—Fiction. I. Title.
   PS3555.L61565 C64 2001
   813'.6—dc21

                                    00-064031

Bill Coffey has generously given permission to use the painting *Kentucky Serenity*
   by Paul Sawyier on the cover
Cover and book design by Paulette Livers-Lambert
Book composition by Lyn Chaffee
Author photograph by Kay Adick

For my father, George Elbert Ellis (1928–1998),
my mother, Mary Cecilia Brell Ellis,
and for Debbie, who always knew I could.

". . . if you're lucky, a place will shape and cut and bend you, will strengthen you and weaken you. You trade your life for the privilege of this experience—the joy of a place, the joy of blood family; the joy of knowledge gotten by listening and observing."

—Rick Bass, *The Sky, the Stars, the Wilderness*

"Later I began to understand that when you have lived with the land as long as they had, if you're lucky, there comes a point when the land is part of you and you are part of it. The union, if not perfect, is inexorable. It's in you, all its rich bounty, its pain and loss, like blood and tissue."

—Harry Middleton, *The Earth Is Enough*

CONTENTS

FOREWORD

It's been said by the late John Gardner and others that there are but two stories in the world: a man or a woman goes on a journey, or a stranger rides into town. Certainly this memoir by Ron Ellis contains a living narrative of the former, though with a perspective that is increasingly rare: the tale of two people, a boy and a man, returning again and again not to any place of new-found experiences, but instead to a tested and beloved landscape.

Under any scrutiny, the structure of this book will seem simple, not complex. But within its pages run enough themes, alternating and repeating, that without trying, a strong and supple braid has been created. One of the dominant braids is the gap or disparity between the father's familiarity with a landscape and its culture, and the son's slowly accruing experience with this same place. Other braids help hold together the simple, elegant structure. Obviously, *Cogan's Woods* is a portrait of one very specific place, 207 acres in Belden County, Kentucky, and one fairly specific time, the early 1960s; but within this little picture-frame of place and time is the small but deep country where childhood, imagination, and memory—always memory—intersect and combine. Reading these pages, particularly those passages that are so keenly attuned to the physical senses, there is very much the feeling that this story possesses no conscious shape of man's construction, but is instead shaped of a form as natural as the flow of a creek across the landscape itself, directed by a destiny as sure as gravity: that destiny being a deep and indestructible bond with the land.

The result is a steady, riverine sense of narrative, memory, and landscape. One can read the current from the very first page in which the father and son are journeying yet again to the place that makes them feel most whole; and we can clearly see how from the foundation of considered ritual and repetition comes meaning. There is a wonderful unselfconscious intensity in the focus upon the physical senses, particularly to the nuances of odor, and to their effect upon the templates of memory. The "damp and thick" swirling odors of "summer and road tar," cigarette smoke and fog: these odors braid, as do the other elements, carrying the boy along into the new world that had already been for so long his father's old world. The scent of the car's undercarriage, warm from its long journey from the city, brushing its hot iron belly against the autumn-dry grass; the residue of the spent powder of gunshells; and of the forest itself after a cool rain.

Nor are the other senses ignored. With similar intensity and lucidity the child notices the green and blue cartridges used in the taking of their quarry; the luminosity of fog; the sight of starlight on steel rails; and the blood-red muscle of the squirrels. Weaving into the memory too is the taste of the

Barq's lime sodas, crisp bacon, fried ham sandwiches on rye with yellow mustard and big slices of sweet onion, Snickers bars, strong black coffee, and "plump, dark tomatoes, almost a deep purple, that were still warm and tasted of the sun."

Strengthening the braid too is another of the primal or elemental components—the stories of others, told well, incorporating themselves both into the developing future memory of the narrator as well as educating him about the past: his past, or his father's past, which in some sense was his—Ron's—long before he ever saw it.

It's too much to ask or hope for, that all such 207-acre patches of woods and prairie and forest and family be given the loving and lyrical attention that Ron Ellis has given in this portrait. And even as we enjoy the telling of it, there creeps into the reader's consciousness at times the fear or suspicion, or even the knowledge, that far too many places have become all but void of such an attached and significant memory among their human inhabitants.

But the act of remembering is above all a celebration of cherished things—friendship and family, storytelling and nature, the physical senses, and the beauty of permanency existing right next to stunning impermanency. The brevity of such things in any individual's life is all the more reason for noticing them, and celebrating them, as Ellis has done here so well.

RICK BASS

ACKNOWLEDGMENTS

I am grateful to Jim Pruett for his belief in me and in this story from the very beginning, and for ultimately wanting to publish this book. Thanks also to everyone at Pruett Publishing, particularly Kim Adams and Chrystal Prentice.

I am grateful to Rick Bass for his love of stories, especially this simple tale, and for penning the foreword of this book; for his guidance at the University of Montana's 1998 Environmental Writing Institute (EWI) at the Teller Wildlife Refuge in Corvallis, Montana; for his enthusiasm and counsel as the manuscript matured; and for his continuing friendship.

Thanks to Professor Hank Harrington of the University of Montana for admitting me to the EWI based on the early pages of this book as a work-in-progress. A special thanks to my twelve friends and colleagues at the EWI for their contributions: Laura Marsh Bell, Eugene Bender, Paul Bogard, Alice Crawley, Sherry Devlin, Susi Klare, Cynthia Perkins, Renee Ripple, Judith Scheffler, Lee Schweninger, Tiffany Trent, and Jennifer White. And thanks to Chris Miller and everyone at Teller Wildlife Refuge, especially Roberta, Linda, Sharon, and Mary, for taking care of us and providing all those great meals during our all-too-brief stay in Montana. This story carries all of your spirits.

I am grateful to Nick Lyons for taking an early interest in this story and to Bill Coffey for the use of the beautiful cover painting by Paul Sawyier. Thanks also to my good friend Kay Adick for the author photograph—she made a fine image, with limited subject matter with which to work, except for Maude, of course.

Thanks to Dianne Nelson for her editorial guidance, to Carolyn Hughes Lynn of the Kentucky Department of Fish and Wildlife Resources for the research assistance, and to Dr. James Ramage for his Civil War anecdotes.

My acknowledgments would be incomplete without a deep expression of love and thanks to my wife, Debbie, for her belief in me as a writer well before the first word of this story was ever written, and to my son, Zachary, for his encouragement and for retrieving this manuscript from a trash pile in cyberspace, after I accidentally placed it there during final revisions.

A special thanks is due my mother, Mary Cecilia Brell Ellis, for her help with the writing of this book. I wish also to acknowledge the support of my three sisters—Beverly Fowee, Anita Scharfenberger, and Lisa Ellis.

Thanks to my many friends and colleagues for their advice, their support, and their contributions, often in the form of snatched pieces of conversation, some of which found its way into this story and into the mouths of its characters. You know who you are, and I hope you know how grateful I am for your friendship and encouragement.

To those people who lived in and around the country that spawned this fictionalized memoir, I send heartfelt thanks for contributing, either in real life or in stories and legend, to so many of my boyhood memories, for providing me with a sense of place for the heart that still endures, and for enriching a time in my life when August days passed slowly and I was permitted a boy's life surpassed by none.

And finally, to Dad. Thank you for Cogan's Woods and for so much more.

1

UPRIVER

When I was young it happened every year. I waited for it, felt I could not live without it, and was never disappointed. It was always in August at the edge of dawn, and when it had rained in the night the fog drifted up from the low places beside the road. My father threaded the old white Mercury through the twists and turns of the crumbling river road as we listened to the weather report coming up from a station in Cincinnati. We always hoped for wet weather, for a soft, steady rain to soak the woods and soften the paths we would soon be traveling in Cogan's Woods. We were heading upriver, on an annual journey to hunt squirrels on opening day among the big trees that stood watch over the country where our hearts lived.

As the car purred and swayed its way east toward Belden County, Kentucky, we munched on peanut rolls and sipped White Castle coffee and hot chocolate from blue and white paper cups, the kind with the folding cardboard handles. The glow of the blue light coming off the Mercury's instrument panel lit the creases in my father's face, and the ash of his cigarette, the size and shape of a pencil eraser, glowed red in the dark interior of the car. Dad steered the Mercury through the advancing gray and talked of other days spent in just this way. "This is a perfect day for squirrel hunting," he said. "Now if the wind will just lie down at daylight, we'll have a good calm, wet day."

The fog thickened as the road twisted back toward the river and sheets of mist doused the light from the low beams, slowing our progress. And then the road turned back toward the hills, the sweep of the headlights revealing pockets of tired land where the skeletal remains of outbuildings stood as lonely reminders of the life that had once been lived there. I opened the "cozy wing" on my side of the car to check the temperature, to see if the weather was going to be just right for the coming hunt. With the little triangle-shaped window pushed open, the night air—damp and thick and smelling of summer and road tar—rushed in and swirled around our faces, pushing the cigarette smoke out the window on my father's side until it joined the fog ghosting above the Ohio River north of the road.

While squirrel hunting was the major focus of this upriver journey, I also enjoyed the chance to spend some time with my father when he seemed to be free of life's pressures. On these trips, there was never a cross word said between us. Just the two of us: father and son, teacher and student, travelers and hunters.

Dad kept the Mercury pointed east, toward Belden County, as I huddled close to the radio and tried to coax in a new signal. We talked about shotguns and squirrel hunting and how we would like to see a deer, a rarity at that time in this part of Kentucky. And we talked about how good it would be to see Sherm and Stony Morgan, the twin brothers who owned the 207 acres known to us as Cogan's Woods, and many other friends and characters who lived in and around those woods. But we talked mostly about this country that we loved and that we would be a part of again, if only for a short time, commuters that we were.

Our conversation was filled with concern about favorite hickory trees, which were found in abundance and in various shapes and sizes in Cogan's Woods. Would the squirrels be cutting the nuts in the crooked-limb hickory that hung over the line fence where the trail came down off the ridge below the barn? Would there be nuts this year on the slender pignut hickories ringing the covered well where an old house had stood so long ago? Would the squirrels be "working" in the trees that bordered the path leading into the big silver beeches that protected and cooled Hickory Nut Grove? Or would there be any hickory nuts at all? Would there be more gray squirrels or fox squirrels in the woods this year? There were always more gray squirrels in the big woods. The heavy-bodied fox squirrels, with coats that glowed bright reddish-orange when illuminated by the sun in the tops of the tallest trees, preferred the large shagbark hickories that stood like sentries along the barbed-wire fences at the edge of the woods or out in the long, narrow meadows, which had been cleared before the turn of the century to make room for burley tobacco and cows.

Our journey on the old river road—now mostly forgotten and seldom traveled due to the completion of a new "superhighway"—took us through Maysville, or Limestone Point as it was known when our ancestors first unloaded their possessions from a flatboat there on the Ohio River in April 1795. Maysville was where both my father and I had been born, and I loved passing through this historical river town in the predawn drape of quiet as its inhabitants slept. It always felt so ceremonial, this creeping through the streets, as if we were showing some deep respect for those ancestors by remaining as silent as we could during our passage.

We drove slowly, past Maysville's famous tobacco warehouses and the big homes and the neat row houses and shops. Every image was reflected in the car windows as we rolled through the streets, the tires ticking against the warm pavement, with a few neon signs beyond the radio station lighting the creases of the town as it spread out toward the dark ridges of the higher ground upriver.

We slipped out the east side, past the entrance to the cemetery on the river side of the road and the long row of clean, white tobacco warehouses with their green roofs opposite it. The edges of the night held fast beyond the reflection of the last of the few streetlights, their shiny glare spilling onto the pavement and mixing with the high beams of the headlights. It was so quiet, so very quiet.

Once beyond Maysville, the twisting two-lane blacktop stretched out before us, dark and capped with patchy fog and running through a string of little towns that were made up of a general store with gas pumps out front and a white, wooden country church with a graveyard. There were also numerous two-story farmhouses, each with whitewashed trees bordering a driveway that was normally no more than two dirt tracks separated by a grassy center. It would inevitably lead to an outbuilding with a drooping basketball rim bolted above its doors and a yard light to spot it hung in a nearby tree. The bare ground closest to the hoop was worn flat and smooth by the endless dribbling of basketballs by countless numbers of kids and by many grownups anxious to show the youngsters they could still make the long shot and play that Kentucky "string music." I imagined them yelling and laughing after dinner out on those courts on warm summer evenings, the men in their bib overalls and heavy work boots playing a few pickup games with the kids in their jeans and high-top canvas basketball shoes.

The town we loved most was White House, because it was the last one we went through before leaving the main highway. The townspeople were still asleep as we passed beneath the dripping canopy of whitewashed maple trees that lined both sides of the road. The only visible light was a gooseneck lamp, with its bare bulb hanging above the front door of the Christian church, its white clapboard bell tower always newly painted and its lawn freshly mowed. This was our navigational light in the darkened and quiet town, at the junction where we turned onto the road that led to Cogan's Woods and where we left the last real town behind in the fading red mist of the Mercury's taillights.

We soared along, looking out over the hood ornament—there was Mercury out there with his arm extended—and we waited for the hands of our watches to travel those long twenty minutes it would take to reach our destination. While this road was still paved with blacktop, it had a different feel to it. It was more pebbled and uneven than the main highway, and it sounded more rural, more distant. The air out there along its shoulders smelled of cows and aging tobacco barns and country gardens ripe with tomatoes and corn. The road was bordered by the best the earth had to offer, or so we believed, and we never failed to recognize just how unique and important those sounds and smells were to us. My father was a master at noticing these things, the "little things" that made a life rich. He seemed to always know what would be important to me *before* it was actually important to me—and never was it more important to underscore their significance than when we were on this annual journey. After two miles into the country on this road, we made a mandatory "convenience stop" next to a large tobacco barn—Dad called it the "Pee Barn"—and after more than eighty miles of secondary roads and many cups of coffee and hot chocolate, the reason for its name was obvious.

The brief stretch of flat road ended here, and just over the lip of the hill the road began a series of twists and turns as it descended toward Cedar Creek. Off in the night were the lights of farmhouses and the sounds of barking dogs, as only dogs can sound in the country in the dark, and the soft lowing of the cows from hillside pastures. Back inside the car, we would go on some more about how lucky we were to have such a fine place to come to each season, and how it felt better with each passing year.

My heart beat faster as the car rolled on toward the turnoff to Cogan's Woods. I counted the hills as we topped them and waited to see the old foxhunters' lodge off to the left of the road. And then there was the yellow road sign that foretold of a stretch of twisted pavement just ahead. It was a black serpentine warning with a well-placed bullet hole serving as an eye in the painted serpent's arrow-shaped head, cautioning us to slow down. The road beyond, its shoulders cracked and peeling and studded with more yellow signs warning drivers to proceed with care, twisted and turned back on itself before climbing a steep hill and descending into a deep hollow. At that point, the country changed drastically. The road narrowed to one lane as we slowed to pass through a natural gateway of crumbling limestone cliffs, the rocky litter nearly scraping the sides of the car.

Just beyond was a dense stand of ancient hardwoods that pressed toward the shoulders of the road, creating a tunnel. Tacked on one old sentry—a towering, peeling sycamore that was rimmed by a shaggy cedar forest so dark and thick that it closed out the world behind the Mercury—was a rusted metal sign printed with the words: "Home of the Undefeated Persimmon Gap Bobcats." Two gentle curves past that sign was the turnoff to the rutted gravel road that led to the Morgan brothers' farm, which is where we entered Cogan's Woods.

The road was paved with washboard ruts and ridges and slick muddy places, with holes deep enough to bog down the low-slung Mercury and keep us from reaching the woods before daylight. And so Dad drove slowly, painful as it was for us not to be able to race toward the big trees in the distance, and eased the car through the bad spots, including a huge, frame-scraping slab of tilted rock that stood guard over the confluence of Pig Pen and Rattlesnake Hollows. These were legendary places where, according to the stories, many colorful characters had hunted and routinely killed their limits of squirrels, a great feat not to be taken lightly in this country, especially in a boy's mind.

My father had grown up here and had learned to hunt in this marvelous country. He spoke of these woods with great reverence and of his love for the places they protected: centers of heavy silence, thick with tradition and a sense of mystery that you could see in the faces of the people who lived here and that you could feel in the light that traveled down through the trees and splashed onto the ground along the woods trails where there were piles of rocks the old-timers called "Indian mounds." While Dad took me to Belden County primarily to teach me to hunt, I believe he wanted, as much as anything, to share with me his love of the woods and to introduce me to the people he cared for so deeply, hoping I would learn to love them and their quiet ways as much as he did. He need not have worried.

What was it that smelled so wonderful when traveling those country gravel and dirt roads in the summer just before dawn that I can remember it still? I could always smell the weeds, mostly the goldenrod that brushed against the side of the car as we passed through the narrow places, and I could smell the tobacco that grew in every field along those ridges. And there was the smell of wood smoke and of breakfast being cooked in the kitchens of the old farmhouses where tired, weathered men were shaking the sleep from their eyes while lacing up a familiar pair of worn leather boots and finishing a final cup of coffee before beginning the day's chores. There were other smells, too, not so easily defined as those coming from outside the car. I believe these other smells came from the blending of a genuine excitement for the hunt and the journey, along with the smell of the equipment and the provisions we carried with us: canvas shell vests, leather boots, coffee and donuts, insect repellent (the mosquitoes in those humid August woods were nasty!), and that greatest smell of all hunting smells—the aromatic scent of Hoppes No. 9.

I believe it was all of those things, mixed with the excitement of wondering if there would be enough squirrels feeding in the tall, shagbark hickories so that both Dad and I could each shoot a limit of six. A limit was important to me. It was something I worked toward and desired more than anything else in the world. I longed to have six squirrels hanging on my belt—three grays and three fox squirrels—each one threaded by a back foot onto the big brass laundry pin with the number "110" stamped on its clasp.

I imagined that if I could kill that mythical limit in Cogan's Woods, the Morgan brothers, catching sight of us returning to the house, would flash their big welcoming smiles while Stony would say, "We thought you boys might be up, now that the law's come in."

I would smile and remove the pin from my belt and hold the squirrels up high so that both Sherm and Stony could admire them. Dad would be proud, too, of his son the hunter as we passed through the peeling locust gateposts into the yard and walked the stone path to the edge of the big front porch.

"Come on up here and sit down," Sherm would say. "I see you have some stories to tell."

2

DAYBREAK

I can never remember being late for a hunt. We may have been late for everything else in our lives, but we were never late for opening day. Maybe once or twice we were delayed in getting away from home so that we found ourselves hurrying along, in a race with the sun to reach the ridge top. But we always made it on time, with the Mercury rolling to a stop where the road ended, right in front of the old two-story white frame house with the big front porch that the Morgan boys called home. We sat there listening to the soft ticking of the Mercury's engine as it cooled down after the long run upriver. The woods, stretched out along the spine of the ridge that ran for more than a mile to the east, straight to the town of Persimmon Gap, were still black smudges against a developing gray sky, floating out there above Mercury on the hood. There was no mistaking the sound or the feel of it all.

Often, Stony's voice greeted us from out of the darkness. He would have seen our headlights coming down the road as he sat there on the front porch in the dark smoking his first cigarette of the day and sipping a cup of thick black coffee.

"Mornin', boys," he would yell. "Thought you might be up today. Good wet day to hunt." He would leave the porch and make his way to the car through the damp grass and the darkness, juggling a big white coffee mug in his left hand, and extend his free hand to Dad. They would shake and then Dad would pour himself a cup of coffee from the red thermos. They would both lean against the car and talk some in low voices and sip at their coffee and smoke, until Stony decided it was time to let us go.

"The light's comin' fast. You'd best be gettin' in the woods. Don't let me keep you. Come up to the house before you go. Sherm'll want to see you." He would retrace his steps to the house and retreat through the screen door into the rectangle of yellow light that was the kitchen. The last sound was of the screen door slapping shut against the door frame, the big spring resonating in the dark.

In the car trunk—we called it the "boot" in those days— Dad kept the shotguns in green canvas cases. We had a pair of sweet little .410 pumps—a Sears Roebuck Ted Williams model for me and Dad's dream gun, a Winchester Model 42. The guns were stored on top of a big cardboard box, which was neatly filled with the important things we would need for the day's hunt: boxes of shotgun shells, canvas shell vests, the dependable army canteen snug in its worn and faded green canvas sleeve, extra socks, olive drab cotton bandanas, cigars, and Snickers bars.

The taking of the gear from the trunk was done with a great deal of ceremony. Dad poured himself another cup of coffee from the thermos, lit a cigarette, then stood quietly for a few moments just studying the darkness and listening. Though I was close by, I suspect he was, during those brief moments, very much alone with his memories and with familiar sounds and voices I could not hear. We spent some time loading our vests with shells—green Remington shells for me and blue Peters hulls for Dad—and taking care in assembling the rest of our equipment. We sprayed the tops of our green canvas caps and the cuffs of our pants and shirts with insect repellent, as much to discourage ticks (or so we thought) as the mosquitoes. Dad finished his last cup of coffee and another cigarette as we stood there in the dark.

We traded shotgun shells, without fail, before going into the woods on every hunt. It was a good-luck ritual, a wish for a successful and safe hunt. We placed the "good-luck shells," which is what Dad called them, into the magazines of the .410s and pumped them into the chambers, the little guns clicking and throwing metallic echoes into the hills that came back to us in the dark. And then we were ready.

We went into the big woods behind the barn by crossing through a low-hanging barbed-wire fence that was just three loose rusting strands stretched between a fence post on the right and a head-high tree limb attached to an old hay barn on the left. This limb had been cut from the Osage orange trees that grew along the pasture on the river side of the woven-wire fence, and it had been worn smooth by much handling over the years. The height and the position of the wire remained constant year after year, and once there was white deer hair wedged between the barbs. It was satisfying to know a deer had traveled through those woods, stopping at the fence, as we always did, listening and studying the woods ahead, testing the air, then crossing the wire and leaving a tuft of hair, the only sign of its passing. Once we passed through the wire, the trip home seemed complete. We could begin to hunt seriously, focusing our attention on the woods and listening for the whoosh! of sweeping tree limbs as squirrels made their way from den trees to feeding areas.

We stood perfectly still in the darkness, listening to rainwater dripping from the trees and watching for light on the eastern horizon. We speculated, in whispers, on how many squirrels we might see and wondered if we would be lucky enough to have the river fog blanketing the ridges to hide our movements until well after first light. The fog up there hung close to the ground out in front of us. The stuttering rhythm of cowbells drifted up from the meadows below as the animals grazed along through the steep pastures. I stood perfectly still and listened and wished again that nothing here would ever change and that this moment I lived for all year long would remain as sweet as it was for as long as I needed it. It was exciting, always, to see the day developing, like a photograph appearing in the white of the developer tray, glimpses of light and distorted black blobs at first, and then the whole image taking form out of a crack of light tracing the tree line to the east.

Then we heard the squirrels jumping through the rain-soaked foliage as they left their den trees—large, brooding beeches down below us, their lightning-struck tops jutting up like broken, decaying teeth—then moving along a network of limbs ("traveling" is what we called it) toward the nut trees. We could see the squirrels as they came closer, jumping from tree to tree, bridging the sometimes incredibly long distances between the trees with their outstretched bodies, then becoming specks, just dark silhouettes, moving silently along through the tops of the tallest trees. We waited to see which direction they were headed, trying to determine the trees they might be feeding in before we moved any farther along the trail. At this point in the hunt, I always imagined Daniel Boone standing there on the same ridge, squirrel rifle in hand, waiting to "bark" a squirrel from a hickory limb at fifty paces with a musket ball.

I had heard the old-timers say during their front-porch story sessions at the Persimmon Gap General Store that "Boone damn sure had hunted up in those woods." I believed it, too, because I was sure I could feel the ancient rhythms and detect another presence in the woods. The old-timers said it was so and that it had been told to them when they were young by the old folks who knew about these things.

In August, the squirrels were feeding mostly on hickory nuts in Cogan's Woods, which was filled with old shagbark hickories along the ridge tops and fence lines. Slender, tight-barked pignut hickories were in greater numbers along the flats and at the edges of clearings. The larger nuts of the shag-barks made loud, soft thumps in the earth when dropped from the highest limbs of the tallest trees by feeding squirrels. It was a cherished sound, one that was heard in the ears long after the season had closed, especially in winter when snow-muffled dreams were filled with the expectations of the coming season. When "cutting a nut," the squirrel's teeth—long incisors capable of reducing the tough husks of hickory nuts to fine litter—made a familiar squeaking sound that never failed to put smiles on our faces. When we heard it, we listened more intently and tried to mark the exact tree where the squirrels were feeding. Once located, we moved on, with greater care and concern for where we placed our feet.

I always followed in Dad's boot tracks in the early days. It seemed I spent more time watching his back and trying to guess when he would stop so I would not stumble over his feet and make enough noise to run off all the squirrels in Belden County. He always had a smile on his face when he had located the feeding areas. He would turn toward me and point his right index finger toward his ear, pretend to cut a hickory nut, then point up toward the trees ahead of us. His next motion would be a finger placed silently before his lips, finished off with a grin and, likely as not, his hand fishing for a smoke in his shirt pocket. Dad often smoked a big black Ibold cigar on these hunts, and its heavy, strong smoke drifted back over his shoulder and across my brow, lingering and mixing with the heavy dampness in the morning air. I could see the smoke and watch the paths it took on the air currents, and it was easy to see how scent could travel in so many different directions in the woods.

Walking the trails in silence was a skill not easily learned, particularly in those years when drought made the leaves so dry and crumbly it felt like we were trying to sneak along on a bed of potato chips. These trails we traveled had known, no doubt, the cautious, careful steps of Indian moccasins. As a kid of the 1950s, I was more than familiar with the Indians' legendary stealth. This was something known to every boy in Kentucky, whether from the many tales told to us by our parents and grandparents, or through the TV exploits of Fess Parker as the legendary pioneers Davy Crockett and Daniel Boone. It was known, too, in local legends that these same trails, which offered commanding views of the Ohio River and the valley below, had served as travel routes for parties of Indians during incursions into the "dark and bloody ground," as "Caintucke" was sometimes called back then, to hunt or to slow the influx of settlers floating down the Ohio in flatboats to reach river ports to the west.

We drank silently of the sounds and smells of the country we had dreamed about and yearned for so many nights downriver. I loved the fresh smell and look of the woods, especially after a morning rain, with the newly washed grasses of the fields a brilliant green and the abandoned rusted farm equipment shoved tight against the tree line, looking as if it were resting in the shadows that ran out from the woods, traveled into the meadows, and lipped away over the ridge to the railroad tracks and the river below. We stood there for as long as it took us to feel satisfied, and then we moved farther into the woods through a passageway of wet foliage. We emerged beneath a dripping canopy of hickory, wild cherry, and maple.

Dad was a sentimental man with a great heart. His whole life, or so it seemed to me, was an honest attempt to illuminate for me some of the best things in life, at least as he saw them— those little things in a person's life that went mainly unnoticed and unappreciated by so many people. He loved to point out the names of the trees and plants we encountered in Cogan's Woods. There were many, and he knew most of them: ginseng, staghorn sumac, wild grapes, ferns, beech, ash, wild cherry, poplar, hickory, blackberry and raspberry canes, devil's tooth-brush, persimmon trees, and pawpaw patches, to name a few of his favorites. His eyes danced when he talked about the plants and the trees and about the people he had shared these woods with over the years. I was injected with his enthusiasm for the telling, and I listened with my heart.

On one particularly wet morning, the squirrels were cutting on large green hickory nuts—the kind with deeply etched lines that quarter the husks and smell so strongly of wet greenery in the damp morning air—and we could hear the squirrels making all this noise from a long way off. As we crept closer, I saw that the top of the largest hickory was "alive" with squirrels. The highest branches of the tree scratched at the sky and stood in a group of three old shell barks—their bark old and loose, peeling away from the trunk and turning up at the ends. I counted five gray squirrels before they began crossing over each other and jumbling up the count, just one short of that mythical limit I was always chasing. Those squirrels were cutting so furiously that the hull litter sounded like a fine rain coming down through the hickory's broad green leaves.

"It's raining," Dad said, a big grin on his face. "You ready?"

"Sure," I said, smiling back. I thought that surely he could hear my heart beating through my shirt and shell vest.

"We'll split up and cover both sides of the tree—you on the right over there and me over here."

"Shoot the lowest one first?" I asked.

"Always. But make sure it's high enough off the ground to be safe. Higher . . ."

". . . than a tall man's head topped with a top hat," I said, finishing one of his favorite rules.

Dad smiled and raised the thumb of his right hand. The woods were noisy now. A blue jay squawked in the top of a beech tree, a church bell rang in Persimmon Gap, and a rooster crowed from across the river.

The squirrels were so busy with their feeding that we slipped through the woods and were almost on top of them before one of them saw us and began barking, cracking its tail furiously while hanging on the side of the biggest hickory. He was up high enough to offer a safe shot. He left the tree on my side, and the .410 pump went to my shoulder. At the shot, he tumbled out of the sky in the middle of a leap, hitting the earth just after the slender blue paper hull, my "good luck shell," was ejected into the leaves. The rest of the squirrels scattered and either attempted to leave the tree or to hide. They flattened their bodies out along the limbs, almost becoming the bark as their skin pressed tightly to it. Dad took the next one as it leaped from the very top of the tree, its body crumpling short of the freedom offered by the nearby limbs of another hickory. The third one decided to hide. Dad killed that one as it hunched in the crotch of two large limbs, thinking it would go undetected so silent was it except for the movement of its tail, the very edges of the downy fur ruffling ever so lightly in the morning breeze. It was enough.

The fourth one popped around my side of the tree. I made a quick shot that surprised both me and the squirrel, as the young gray dropped and lay motionless at the base of the tree. I pumped another shell into the chamber and missed the fifth squirrel as it ran out on a low limb headed for the safety of a nearby oak. He leaped from the side of the oak and ran out through the leaves down over the hill. I heard him bounding off in the dry leaves—never stopping, never looking back. Then there was a strange stillness, the kind of quiet that comes after so much noise and commotion in once-quiet woods.

We gutted the squirrels with our pocketknives, poured water from the canteen into the exposed cavities, and wiped the red-muscled meat with folded paper towels. We threaded the squirrels onto our brass laundry pins and snapped them to our belts. The squirrels hung down and bumped against the front of our legs, staining our pants with flecks of dark red. We buried the towels with the entrails in the loose soil in the woods and covered the place with downed tree limbs.

"This is a good feeling," Dad said. "Yet, I always want to put them back in the trees so that I can come back another day and find them just the way we found them today." He picked up his beloved Winchester and slipped two fresh Peters shells into the magazine. He checked the safety and cradled the shotgun in the crook of his left arm. From his pants pocket he pulled out one of the spent shells, the green Remington "good-luck shell" I had given him that morning, and rubbed it between his thumb and forefinger. As always, he held it to his nose and sniffed at the powder residue, as if by doing so he could keep the recent memory close, a reminder of a good day with its bittersweet moments.

"Let's sneak into the Grove," Dad whispered. He pocketed the shell and bent under a low-hanging limb of a young hickory that was heavy with the morning's rain. Water ran off the leaves, and an orange spider clung to the center of its web, which was dotted with hundreds of tiny, clear beads of water. Dad pushed the limb aside and held it back for me to pass, then returned it to its former position. I looked back at the spider and saw that it was making repairs to the web, which had been damaged with the bending of the limb. The spider continued to work, and we slipped along the wet path, our eyes raised to the first light raining down through the tallest trees.

3

INTO THE GROVE

Sacred earth, this ground we called Hickory Nut Grove—a place so revered that I felt I should genuflect before entering—from its foyer of ancient beech trees with their silvered trunks and brushy, gray-green canopy, to its interior, its heart, where hickory trees cast long shadows along the trail for one thousand of my steps. I know it was that many steps from the time we entered the Grove until we reached its far side, because I counted them on one trip we made through there in the rain. We were not hunting, just passing through and trying to keep from getting soaked, and I counted each step as we moved along the soggy path. This was the last place we hunted in the morning, on every trip. If squirrels were scarce elsewhere in Cogan's Woods—as they sometimes were when the mast crop was thin or nonexistent—this place, this cathedral of quiet green and diffused light, was guaranteed to provide at least a sighting of some game.

The big beeches edged both sides of the path that ran down through the middle of the woods, worn smooth by the cattle that had roamed in there since before the turn of the century. Sneaking along undetected beneath the great trees was easier than in most other places. It was easy going the whole way, with the underbrush pruned back by the cattle so as not to rustle against your pant legs. There were no blow-downs littering this trail, no brushy tangles to avoid, and no low limbs crisscrossing the path to make it easy to bang a shotgun barrel against, destroying the silence of the stalk. This was as clean and wide open as the cover got in Belden County.

"I like hunting these woods more than any others," Dad always said. "They're pretty, and they always hold squirrels. Besides, I've never seen a snake anywhere in here." Snakes, particularly copperheads and rattlers, were always a major concern.

"When I was a kid," Dad said, "I was climbing up out of a hollow one time in August. It was hot and dry, and real still. At the end of this ravine, I had to scale up the side of a shale bank to get out of the woods. To do that I had to lay my gun on a ledge above my head so that I could use both hands to pull myself up. When I unloaded my gun and laid it up there, I heard this hissing sound real close to me. I never saw it, but it sounded like a rattler. I just eased my gun back toward me and nearly fell down into that ravine getting out of there."

Snakes. There was no love lost between us. None at all.

Not far from where we entered the Grove there was a huge beech, maybe the oldest and the biggest in all of Cogan's Woods. It had stood watch over this ground well before Dad had started to hunt here. It was a favorite "initial tree," its smooth, gray bark an inviting canvas that was friendly to a boy with a pocketknife and some time on his hands. Three generations of Ellis boys had carved their initials there, one below the other, a legacy of sorts, each taking the time to confirm their passing. Years later, my mother would accompany Dad on a hunt to these woods, and he would carve her initials in that tree as well, one of his many tributes to her, his life's greatest passion. Legend had it that in these same woods, both Boone and Kenton had carved their names. I looked through most of this forest for their initials, studying the sides of each tree for any carvings as I passed by, but I never could find a trace of them. I imagined those famous carvings to be there, forever a part of the woods marking the passing of others, and like a boot track in the mud, they were sharp when first made, but then faded as years of wind and water and sun slowly erased the detail. They were my undiscovered forest treasure, and like a prospector, I would keep searching for them for years among those trees.

We encountered only two other humans in all of the years we hunted there. The first was another hunter from a nearby county who had come to know the people who owned a farm bordering the woods close to the river. They had invited him to hunt anytime, he told us. On this particular day, he had drifted up into the Grove from the woods below. At dawn, he told us, he had set up against a big beech to watch a hickory that was hanging full of nuts, with a layer of fresh cuttings beneath it. That's when he saw the fox.

"This old red fox come to me out of the fog," he said as he produced the dead fox from behind his back and held it out in front of him by the tail so we could clearly see his accomplishment. "I cut down on him with this old Long Tom sixteen. He never even twitched, fellas."

"Foxes aren't in season, you know," Dad said.

"Don't matter none to me about the law," he said. He held the fox down by his side, its front feet dragging on the ground. I could see its face masked with dried blood, eyes wide open and peering out through the mess.

"What are you going to do with it?" Dad asked.

"Take it up to town, to the store," he said.

"You do that. The folks up in Persimmon Gap would love to see that fox. They're fond of foxes, you know," Dad said.

"Thought maybe somebody'd buy the pelt. It ain't hurt none. I shot him square in the face. Plain as day, you can see that. There ain't a pellet in him nowheres else."

We said a clipped good-bye and passed each other on the path, giving a wide berth to the surly poacher and the dead fox. We continued on toward the back side of the Grove, while he went down over the hill, toward the river and to his rendezvous with the people of Persimmon Gap.

"They'll hang his hide up to dry when he gets there," Dad said. "Those old boys bought a load of foxes some years ago and put them out in this country to run with their dogs. They'll run him off for sure, and he won't have that fox with him either. Goddamn, he'll remember this day the next time he thinks about shooting something out of season."

And then some years after that chance encounter, there was a meeting with another kind of hunter. We discovered him late in the morning on a sun-warmed hillside near the end of the Grove. His name was Granger Nelson and he was a hunter of ginseng, the herb that has been coveted by the Chinese for thousands of years. Dad had only a glimpse of him heading for the shadows under the beeches, but it was enough. He had grown up around the old man who was known throughout Belden County to live just to dig ginseng.

"That you, Granger?" Dad asked. We were standing downhill from where he was hiding against the back side of a big beech. "I know you're huntin' ginseng, like you always have in here. Might as well come out and say hello. It's me, George Elbert."

We eased up the hill and stopped at the edge of a stand of walnut trees. Dad pointed to the ground beneath the trees. We could see the evidence of Granger's probing: the soil and leaf litter were disturbed, as if a flock of feeding turkeys had passed through, mostly in some shady spots next to an area carpeted by close-growing ferns. Granger stayed quiet, still using the shadows to hide his presence and the focus of his searching.

"Granger?" Dad said. "You coming out, or should we just go on?"

The old man slithered around to the front of the beech, keeping his back pressed against its smooth bark. Slung over his left shoulder was an old canvas pouch made from feed sacks, its bottom wet and dirty. He carried no gun, only a walking stick sharpened to a point on one end. This is what he used to probe the forest in his clandestine search for treasure. His clothes were made of patched and faded canvas and were stained by the earth, a near match for the sack. The whole outfit was topped off with a misshapen, dark green felt hat, an owl feather stuck in its rumpled crown, the wide brim shading his face and painting its wrinkles and creases with the shadow-camouflage a ginseng hunter craves.

"George Elbert," the old man said. He leaned against the beech, placed his right foot up on its knobby roots, and nudged back his hat with the thumb of his right hand. "You could let a man be when he's in here huntin', you know. It's not necessary to call him out, like he was some kind of criminal." Granger Nelson was legendary for his love of ginseng and ginseng hunting. Until that day, I had never seen the legend—I'd only heard stories about how he knew more about that magic root than anybody else in Belden County and how he had even gone to college for a year.

"Sorry, Granger. It's the end of the day for us," Dad said. "The woods are getting hot and dry and so we're moving fast to get out to the old road on the back side of the Grove. We need to get back up to the Morgan place by lunch."

"It might not be the end of the day for everybody in these woods," Granger said. He spat into the leaves and chased at it with the stick. "You still with the railroad, like your dad?"

"I am. I live down near Cincinnati now."

"What brings you back home?"

"Squirrels, mostly. We've been coming into these woods from up on the ridge for a number of years now. We hunt the Grove out and then come back in toward the car on top of the ridge."

"That your white car parked up near the barn?"

"Yessir."

"Never had a machine myself. I've always walked, or rode a horse or a train mostly."

"You having much luck with the ginseng hunting?" Dad asked.

Granger Nelson patted the sack at his side and spat again into the leaves. "After all these years, you get to know where gin-sang wants to be," he said. "Lookin' for these roots gets to be a bit more important than the money a man can make from them. It gets in the blood and it's kind of all a man thinks about, except for women, of course. The women, they're always hovering around out there competing with the gin-sang and a drink of good whiskey." Those stories I had heard about the legend also held that Granger drank some, mostly whiskey of unknown origins, and that he was a notorious womanizer. Dad laughed and we moved closer to the old shadow chaser.

"Show my boy what those roots look like, Granger," Dad said.

"You got a name, son?" Granger asked, pointing the stick at me.

"Yessir. It's Ron," I said.

"Ron," he repeated. "That's a good name. I have known your daddy since he was your age. He any better at killing squirrels than he used to be?"

"He's pretty good, sir."

"He ought to be. Spent enough time at it," he said. He spat again and called me closer to his side, close to where the sack hung. He pulled out two of the mud-stained, twisted roots and laid them side by side in the palm of his hand.

"These roots were all wet when they first come up out of the ground. They look a lot like a man, don't they? The older a root is and the more it looks like a human, the more its worth in China. The Chinese words for gin-sang mean that, you know, that the roots look like a man. A Chinaman I met down on the river told me that years ago. He was workin' on a coal barge that broke down and stopped at Persimmon Gap for repairs. I had dug some gin-sang by then but didn't know beans about it really until I met that Chinaman. I sat down there on the barge and listened to him real close, at night, next to a lantern. We sat there and smoked and he talked and pointed at the pages of an old book he had. The writing was in Chinese, so I just listened to him talk in this strange language, halfway between Chinese and English, and point to drawings of gin-sang in that book. He taught me most of what I know about these roots, mostly how to hunt and dry them. He bought all the gin-sang I had at the time, which wasn't much, and showed me where to sell more when I got it. I rode the barge downriver with him when the repairs were done and got off at a houseboat anchored on this side below Cedar Creek. The Chinaman got me acquainted with an old buyer and then went on downriver. Never knew that Chinaman's name and I never saw him again neither. That old river rat he introduced me to bought most of the gin-sang dug in this country for a trader down in Cincinnati. After that, we did a good bit of business, before he died on me a few years back."

Granger put the roots back into the bag and slid it under his arm. He stooped down, leaning on the stick, and motioned for me to join him. He pointed the stick at a ginseng plant close to the beech and continued to tell me about his passion.

"This time of year there's red berries on gin-sang to give it away. A man needs to scatter the seeds in those berries before he digs a plant. Got to make sure there's plenty around for the days ahead, if you know what I mean. You find most of it on the north side of the hill, in the shade. I favor rotten logs and old spring seeps myself. I only dig the older plants. They got to be at least a three-prong like this one before I dig it. You got to hunker down like we are when you're lookin', more like a crawl than a walk, if you want to find much of it. It's a lot like huntin' for morels in the spring. Like I said before, you get to know where it wants to be and you just kind of go there. I can't really explain it much. There's a good bit of magic in all this to be sure," Granger said.

"Like with magicians?" I said.

"No. I'm not talkin' about pullin' rabbits out of hats or any of those kinds of tricks," he said. "I mean, once you get to know something, like this gin-sang I'm always chasin', you learn when and where to look for it. Knowing about the woods, like you do for squirrel huntin', means you can move around real easy like and see things that others can't or won't take the time to see. Finding gin-sang means spendin' a good bit of time in the woods by yourself just lookin' in shadows. Sometimes you find more than gin-sang. Sometimes you find that the woods have a spirit life. Nothin' like ghosts or anything like that, just that out here there are other things, like rhythms all around you that are always changin' with the moods of the country, with the trees and rocks and water. You learn after a while that you're not alone out here much of the time. That Chinaman knew that, and he taught it to me sittin' down on the river at night. That's the kind of magic I mean, son. You understand better now?"

"I think. I'll have to practice it some, though."

"You'll get better at it. I can see it in your eyes. You'll get better real fast." Granger Nelson looked at Dad and smiled. He stood up without much trouble—even at such an old age he seemed young, limber as a dancer, eager to be on his way.

"I may have overstayed my welcome, George Elbert," he said. "I get to talkin' too much sometimes, especially when it comes to gin-sang. It's been some time since I've had such an eager pair of ears. You boys take care." Without any hesitation, he threw up his hand in a quick good-bye and set off down the path, back toward where we had just come from.

"Come out sooner next time when I call to you, Granger," Dad said after him. "We'd have more time to talk, you know. You take care."

The old man's back was arched up inside the canvas coat, and the muddy sack rode up high under his left arm as he reached out with the walking stick. Soon he left the main path and angled off toward the river.

It was a good year for mast with every hickory tree hanging heavy with nuts, and a thick covering of gnawed hulls—a fine litter of cuttings that looked like a layer of gravel—accumulated at the base of their trunks. Many of these nuts had ripened early, and the squirrels had cut them sometime in the week before the season opened. By opening day, the squirrels had moved on to other hickories deeper in the Grove. We, too, moved along quickly, anxious to reach a favorite tree—an ancient hickory with a bent trunk and another hickory growing out of its center—before the squirrels had finished feeding and had left the tree for the cool shelter of a nearby den tree or leaf nest.

The crooked tree leaned over the remnants of a barbed-wire fence off to the right of the path. Dad held up his hand and we stopped in our tracks. I was close to his back and could smell the insect repellent mixed with cigar smoke and the musty scent of his canvas hunting vest. I searched the woods for some clue, some movement that would let me see what he had seen, hear what he had heard. In the top of that crooked hickory, the limbs trembled with the movements of a squirrel gathering a fresh nut to cut. We were fully exposed to him and could never hope to get close enough to take a shot without being spotted. We stood still for the longest time, then Dad shuffled his feet in leaves just off the path. The squirrel froze, deciding to hide and to pretend to be invisible, then stared straight at us. Dad took several quick steps forward to put him within range. The Winchester cracked once, and the squirrel, a large gray with a wide, flat tail, never even heard it.

At the shot, another gray squirrel appeared behind us, clinging to the side of a beech and scolding us for intruding. A sassy barker, he hung there cracking his tail, chattering his alarm. Before I could get the gun to my shoulder, he vanished around the back side of the tree and took to the ground. I heard him loping off through the leaves into the hickory woods beyond.

"My best friend, Denver, killed six squirrels out of this tree with six shots from his 16-gauge single-shot," Dad said as he cleaned the squirrel. "It was a real foggy morning and he only had six shells with him. It was during the war, so shotgun shells were scarce. He told me when he left there were six more squirrels up in that tree cutting. They just kept coming all morning because there weren't many nuts in this country that year."

Dad laughed at the memory.

"Can you imagine that? All those squirrels in that one little crooked tree. I've never seen twelve come into any tree. And Denver never did again either. Not that I know of, anyway."

Many years later I would come back to this exact spot. The crooked hickory was down by then and the woods had been logged, with only a stump field remaining. The land was scarred, completely and grotesquely changed, and the people who had mattered to us were by then long dead or had moved to the comfort of nearby cities. The place was so different, but I wanted to see if the pieces could still fit in such an altered landscape, to see what was there that still belonged to me, that might keep me from abandoning it.

I took a photograph of Dad wandering among the debris, going away from the camera, looking for the old path that led out of the Grove—now laid bare and devoid of any enchantment. His head is bowed and he is cradling his beloved Winchester Model 42 in the crook of his arm. He is walking fast, much faster than he ever did when the woods were big and green and there were squirrels to be hunted and memories to be made.

At the very end of the Grove, there was a small clearing surrounded by a dense thicket of cool, blue-green cedars where we stopped to rest when the sun was nearly straight up, our shirts sweat-stained and the woods dry and noisy. There were patches of ferns in all shades of green, and several springs bubbled up and trickled down through them in the loose black soil. The air felt cool and wet when you placed your hand just above the fronds. By this time of the day, the blue jays were busy knocking beechnuts from high up in the treetops and scolding us with their one-note cries of "flee! flee!" as we passed beneath them.

Dad always made straight for the deep shade, feeling for the army canteen he carried on his right hip. It was his father's canteen, the same one he had drunk from many times in these very woods. He took good care of that canteen, emptying it before we left the woods at dark and shaking it, the chain and cap wedged between his thumb and index finger, until he was sure it was empty. Then he would store it in the big cardboard box in the Mercury's trunk, with the canvas cover unsnapped and the cap laid to one side to help dry it and keep it free of odors, to keep the water sweet.

"Taking this canteen along is like having Grandpa back," he would always say. "The cover even smells like him. I've never washed it since he gave it to me, just because of that."

He always put his hand on his right hip, feeling for the comfort of it, and gave the canteen's cap a safety twist before heading off down the trail, his thirst, and then some, satisfied by the familiarity of it all.

The railroad ran close to the river below this cool refuge. After we were settled beneath the cedars for a brief rest, we could hear the trains passing below us, their horns blaring, the notes flattening and spreading out through the woods and then echoing from across the river as they blasted through Persimmon Gap, where they did not stop for any reason. The railroad no longer favored people as passengers, preferring instead to haul freight—lifeless forms requiring no human comforts. There were no warm smiles from conductors who tucked away pocket watches in their dark blue vests before shouting "all aboard," that sweet command that signaled to travelers and their family and friends that a new journey was about to begin.

We left the coolness of the cedars and climbed uphill to reach the Mercury on an old wagon road that used to lead to Persimmon Gap when horses were the main method of getting about these hills. When cars and trains took over as the primary carriers, the old road was no longer needed and so it disappeared beneath a covering of thick yellow grasses and blackberry tangles. Both sides of it were bordered by more cedars—big brooding trees that cast deep shadows and created cool pockets for game to rest in as the afternoon sun sucked the morning's moisture from the ground. It was there, at the edge of those cedars and shadows, that I saw my first pheasant.

"Did you see him?" Dad said. The bird had exploded at our feet from the base of one of those cedars. "That's a pheasant for you. All jumpy and nervous." There was great excitement in his voice, a kind of passion I had not heard before, not even for the squirrels.

The bird, this pheasant, did not have a white collar around its neck, and there were no bright colors on its head. It did not look like any pheasant I had ever seen on the covers of *Field & Stream* or *Sports Afield.*

"You sure that was a pheasant?" I asked.

"Not a ringneck pheasant," Dad said, "but a grouse. People up here call them pheasants."

"They're fast, whatever they are."

"I've never been able to hit one of those old brown birds. They're up and gone before I can get my gun on them. Lots of guys around Persimmon Gap have, though. My dad killed a few over the years, mostly when he stumbled onto one when quail hunting down near the river in some of those old brushy draws. I always wanted to shoot one for myself so that I could look at it real close when it was still warm and lifelike."

"I'm not sure I could hit one. But I'd like to try," I said.

"There's plenty of them in this country. We'll hunt them together here someday."

In time, I would learn to love to hunt those "old brown birds." Years later this would be the place I came to with Dad, when I had decided to become a serious grouse hunter, to make good on that promise. It was the day before Christmas Eve. We had hunted hard all day without much luck. Lady, my sweet little persimmon and white Brittany with the smiling eyes, had found a bird or two, but we had not been in position to shoot. By late afternoon, we reached the saddle in the ridge above the cedar thicket that sheltered the old wagon road.

"I think I'll stay up here and poke around for a while," Dad said. "You and Lady go on down the road there and see if you can find a bird or two. Just down the hill is where you saw your first pheasant. Remember?"

"Couldn't forget that bird," I said. "It was the first time I heard you call them pheasants."

"I still like calling them pheasants. Guess I always will," he said. "You come back up here and get me on your way out and we'll head back to the car and stop and see Sherm and Stony before dark." He moved on down the ridge and sat on a big rock.

"Are you sure you wouldn't rather hunt?" I asked.

"I'm sure. And be careful. You know these woods about as well as I do by now. Still, you have to be careful. I'll be fine here. I have some remembering to do."

I left him sitting up there on that rock, the corduroy collar of his faded canvas hunting coat turned up against the wind. He was smoking a cigar and looking off toward the river, the hills across it barely visible in the dusky evening air. The barrel of his Ithaca pump gun rested back against his left shoulder. He looked content sitting there, smoking and alone with his thoughts. I wondered how many times he had done just that, at that exact spot.

I spent the next two hours looking for birds. On a flat below where Dad sat on that rock, the ground is composed of soft gray clay littered with chips of gray-green slate. The cedars grow well in that poor ground, and just beyond, toward the river, there is an overgrown pasture, a place where we had seen birds in years past. Lady searched the edges and came up with a scent that worried her. She drifted with it and worked and worked until she decided to point. I whispered to her as I moved to flank her, fully expecting a grouse to blow up in front of me before I could get set for a shot. The spongy ground sucked at my boots on every step, and when I stepped into the cover, a pair of woodcock corkscrewed up through the cedars and the second-growth hardwoods. I lowered my gun, as the woodcock season had been closed for several weeks.

"Not this time," I said to Lady. She looked at me with concern, cocking her head this way and that, as if trying to understand my words, my intentions here, and then the sparkles in her amber eyes danced and I knew she understood. "Hunt 'em up, girl," I said. "Find me a grouse now."

Near the bottom of the hill, I found and killed, over Lady's next point, my first Belden County "pheasant"—not more than 100 feet from the spot where Dad and I had flushed that first one so many years ago. Lady found the dead bird and I dressed it alongside the old road and hung the entrails in the branches of a big cedar to keep them away from her. I placed the bird in my hunting coat and picked up the shell I had used to kill it—a green Remington, number 8 shot—and sniffed at the still-warm scent of the burned powder. Now I loved these woods for yet another reason. "Too many to count," I said to the woods. "Too many to count." I called Lady and headed up the steep hillside to meet Dad. Before I reached the saddle in the ridge, it began to snow. The flakes drifted slowly by, as if in a dream, falling steadily. The woods were becoming covered in white. Nothing stirred. I climbed on.

At the top, just a step over the crest of the ridge, on a narrow shelf of ground that allowed me to look out over a thicket of ancient cedars, I stopped to catch my breath and to see if I could discover which way Dad had gone. I had not been there long before I saw him below me, coming up out of the cedars. The trees had a bluish-green tint in the fading light of the evening, their soft limbs bending with the slowly accumulating snow. Dad was on a game trail that passed through the middle of the cedars and headed straight toward me. A crow, the color of the shiny onyx ring Dad had worn for years, and which he had bought with his first railroad paycheck at the age of seventeen, lifted off from somewhere near Dad and flew directly over my head. As it passed above me, it pulled up its ash-gray feet and tucked them into the blackness of its belly. With its wings slowly flapping, it traveled noiselessly through the heavy winter sky and disappeared in the falling snow, headed into the heart of the Grove.

"Stay up there so you can see down into here," he said. "Call Lady and just stand there and watch."

"You got a bird down there?" I asked.

"No bird, just a surprise."

With his shotgun cradled in his left arm, Dad started back down the path, snow building on the shoulders of his hunting coat and the curled brim of his faded green Jones cap. The light was dim and it was quiet enough that I could hear the click of his Zippo lighter as he walked away from me. I saw a flame move toward a cedar to his right, and then a little flame flickered within the webby green darkness of the cedar limbs.

In seconds, several more tiny flames were flickering there. Then Dad moved to his left and more tiny flames appeared in the tree limbs on that side of the trail. Before he was done, he had passed down through those cedars and lit a hundred or more white candles that he had placed in the branches on both sides of the trail while I was off hunting. The entire thicket was illuminated with white candlelight and more snow was coming down. The whole place looked very much like the inside of one of those glass balls you shake to make it snow, and then the snow settles down on a Currier & Ives Christmas scene. And there was Dad, standing at the far end of the lighted tunnel with a big smile on his face.

"Merry Christmas, son," he yelled. And then he walked back through the candlelit cedar trees and stood next to me on the ridge in the gathering dark.

"I always wanted to do this up here, all of my life," he said. "This place has always felt more like Christmas to me than any place I've ever been. There's just something about the way the hills roll and the way the light comes in here in the evening. It gets all stained with the color of these cedars.

"The first time I came up here was with my father. I was young and we were out looking for a lost rabbit dog that belonged to a friend of his. The dog got to running a fox and ran out of the country. We were at this exact spot when Dad told me to stay put and listen for the dog while he cut through the cedars and went out to the point over there to listen for it."

He looked off toward that place, as if looking again for his father standing out there alone. He waved his hand over the spot before going on with the story.

"Well, while I was standing here looking and listening, I didn't see or hear that hound, but coming up through these cedars on this same trail was a big buck. There weren't many deer in this part of the country then, or now, but the old men told stories about this one big buck that was said to haunt this piece of ground. Well, he came out of the cedars, just down there," he said, pointing to the spot. "His rack was draped with all this shredded greenery, like he'd been rooting around on the ground, and there was this crown of that bright green moss that grows under cedars up here, mixed with what looked like some mistletoe riding on top of his rack. He looked every bit the picture of Christmas." He paused to light his cigar, blew a thick puff of smoke into the sky, then continued.

"That old buck stood there for some time, so I got a good look at him. He was staring right at me and I was afraid to move, afraid he'd leave. Finally he pawed at the ground, snorted in my direction, and then ran off, up toward Sherm and Stony's place, with his long white tail held straight up in the air as he cleared the deadfalls up on that flat of second-growth timber. When he reached the edge of the woods near the pasture, he stopped. He was silhouetted against the sky, the light just about like it is now, and he shook that big rack from side to side and then turned and ran across the pasture. I never saw him again, and I never told my Dad I'd seen that deer. I'm not sure he would have believed me anyway. Before we left that night, I made sure to go down there and look for tracks. I found them right where he had been standing, so I know he really was there. You believe me, don't you, son?" His eyes were clear and there was a good bit of grin on his face as he puffed on the cigar and shook some snow off the collar of his coat.

"Why wouldn't I?" I said.

"I knew you would. You've always been a believer. I'm glad I waited until now to tell you that story and to light up those trees. Merry Christmas, son," he said.

"Merry Christmas, Dad," I whispered, "and thanks for the story."

I showed him the "pheasant" and shared the story of its killing. He patted me on the shoulder, talked to Lady, and reached into his pocket. He gave me a blue Peters .410 shell, a paper one, with a note rolled up inside of it. I fished out the tiny tube of paper, lit my lighter, held the flame above it, and read:

August 30, 1964. Ron killed two gray squirrels and a fox squirrel today with the Sears .410. This was his "good luck" shell. I killed three grays and a fox squirrel out on the point. The weather was wet and foggy. Ron saw his first pheasant. A good day, one to remember.

"I thought since you're a pheasant hunter now you'd like to know when you saw your first one," Dad said. "I thought it was a good Christmas present to give out here in the woods."

I reached into my pocket and handed him the green Remington 20-gauge shell I had used to kill the grouse. "There's no note in, yet," I said. He sniffed at the green paper hull, then rubbed it between his thumb and index finger as he had always done, like he was trying to get all of the experience out of the shell, connecting with it as deeply as possible.

"Make a note to put in it," he said. "Write down the best details so you can remember how it was, when you were happiest. You'll always be glad you did." He gave the shell back to me, pulled his collar up, and adjusted his carry of the shotgun. I glanced at his face and saw his eyes were red, and there was a glisten to them. "The wind's picking up," he said. "Cold, too. All of this weather's got my eyes to watering. We'd better get on back to the car."

We stood there a few minutes longer, reluctant to leave, and watched the tiny flames flickering in all that dark green of the cedars, until the last one had died out. We eased down the steep slope of the ridge and slipped out along the trail. As we passed among the cedars, one more candle, one we had not seen, hissed and gave up its final light to the snow and to the quiet coming of another Christmas in the hills.

4

Nooning Up

When the sun drifted to noon, big and bright and hot, we emerged, reluctantly, from the woods and returned to the Mercury, where cool drinks waited for us. We either ate lunch out in the woods on the back of the farm or made the short drive to buy lunch at the Persimmon Gap General Store. If we planned to stay in Cogan's Woods, we brought food along in a big red Coca-Cola cooler, one of those metal ones with a bottle opener permanently attached to its side. It was heaped with ice and cold drinks—Dr. Pepper for me, Barq's lime soda for Dad, and cold canned Pabst Blue Ribbon beer for Sherm and

Stony. Mom would have been up early to fix our lunch—fried ham sandwiches on rye bread with yellow mustard and big slices of sweet onion, potato chips, and Snickers bars. We always added a couple of ripe tomatoes from the Morgan boys' garden—plump, dark red tomatoes, almost a deep purple, that were still warm and tasted of the sun.

Sometimes we ate out on the porch with Sherm and Stony, if we found them at home, taking a break from their work in the tobacco fields. Their lunch seemed always to consist of crisp bacon—not the thin shavings we called bacon back in the city, but thick, heavy slabs of smoky, lean meat. With the bacon went fresh stewed tomatoes and lots of soft white bread, and a pot of strong black coffee.

"Working in that 'backer patch can make a man mighty hungry," Sherm would say. "One time we had a pet goat by the name of Wimpy. He'd eat anything that weren't tied down, and even that that was sometimes. We'd come in for lunch on this one day and had set out food on the kitchen table when a neighbor come by. We walked out on the porch to chat some and when we come back in, old Wimpy was standin' in the middle of the table grazin'. It was a damn mess. We ate what we could see he hadn't been eatin', which wasn't much. Ever since then, I don't leave my lunch, not for nobody, not for no reason."

If the Morgan brothers were not going to be at home during lunchtime, they would leave a note wedged under the Mercury's windshield wipers to save us a trip to the house. I kept the last one they wrote. Written in pencil on the back of a card issued to trappers by a Cincinnati furrier for marking pelts, it reads: "Sorry Boys but we have to leave early today to meet a neighbor in town. We might be back before you leave but if not come back any time. Stony."

In their absence, Dad drove down the tractor lane that ran out through the pasture along a big tobacco field, with me running ahead and opening the flimsy gates, just three parallel strands of sagging barbed wire attached to two skinned locust limbs, at each "gap." Dad drove out to the back side of the tobacco patch to a spot where long ago woodcutters had left stumps from an abandoned logging operation that now served as our tables and chairs.

We ate out there at the edge of the lane beneath a high canopy of hickory, ash, and wild cherry trees. There was always enough wind moving in the tops of those trees to cool us. Dad sat in the shade, his shirt stained with sweat, telling stories about hunting here as a boy with friends from Persimmon Gap.

They used to gather at the store in the darkness, he said, the stars bright in the sky, leaving town well before daylight. They either hiked out of town through the woods to the west, on the same trail the Indians were said to have used when coming into Kentucky from north of the river, or they walked the railroad, moving fast so as to cover the distance of more than a mile in time to climb uphill into the woods before daylight.

I imagined how it might have felt to be walking along the rails with my father and his friends. There would have been the heavy scent of gravel and creosote, the ancient wood ties splintering between the shiny rails, the stars reflected in them when the moonlight was right as they walked along, side by side, their guns cradled in their arms so the barrels pointed away from each other. There would have been a great silence for long stretches, with talk coming only in whispers, barely audible above the crunching of their boot soles on the warm gravel of the railroad bed. Just before dawn, they would leave the tracks, cross the dirt road, and pick their way up through the steep-tiered pasture that led into Cogan's Woods.

They still-hunted in the early gray of August and then hunted through the Grove at mid-morning, as we always did, then came up over the ridge and took a lunch break at the same spot where we sat, or they nooned-up at a spring that collected in a low place next to the old Morgan homeplace. Sitting there munching on my fried ham sandwich, I wondered about the rest of the Morgan family that lived in that old house under the hill. I knew there was another brother and a sister, both dead at young ages, but I knew very little about the parents. I imagined their mother—her name was Effy—to be the classic hill-farm wife, beginning her days well before dawn and worrying about the kids while doing her seemingly endless chores. I visualized her sitting on the porch of the little house, breaking green beans into a big metal pot while watching the path coming out of the cedars for her husband to return from his farming or from running errands in Persimmon Gap. Or maybe she would look for a friend from town who had come out to visit or for a hunter coming to drink at their spring while traveling between woods. She must have collapsed into her bed late each night and just lay there listening to the night sounds and yearning for something new, something maybe the city had to offer that these old woods could not. And I wondered if she could hear the dripping of the spring as it emerged from the hillside and slowly filled the tiny reservoir beneath it as the moon washed over the star-spattered water on its journey toward dawn.

At this spring, Dad said, there was always a tin cup hanging in a dogwood tree—a cup that could be used by any traveler to dip a cold drink from the clear waters that collected there. We often searched for that spring, raking layers of leaves away with the toes of our boots where Dad said that it should be and poking around with sticks looking for wet, muddy spots a bit deeper in the earth that might provide a clue to its location. We found patches here and there of soft ground—spots that had been covered by years of accumulated forest litter and by a constantly eroding hillside—that suggested a spring might once have bubbled up in those places long ago. I wondered if a spring that had been active for so many years could simply disappear—just go away without leaving a sign, evading all the while our serious detective work. We never found the spring, which is something I always regretted. I wanted to find it and the remnants of that tin cup.

This place where we ate lunch was not far from a pasture where years ago Dad and his best friend had taken shelter in a lean-to during an unexpected rainstorm while on an August squirrel hunt. To stay dry, they huddled beneath this shelter, which had been built by a local farmer, a man they knew, for just such a need. The farmer had been surprised by the storm as well, Dad said, since he was visible to them at the far end of the field, running for the shelter of his house on the hillside below. He had obviously planned to break for lunch at this same lean-to, because hanging from the tree branches of the crude roof above them was his metal lunch pail, which my father and his friend opened to examine the contents. Inside were two biscuits stuffed with country bacon and thick slices of sweet onion, and two ripe tomatoes. Because they had only a canteen of water and nothing to eat, and the storm seemed to be in no hurry to leave, they leaned back and ate the man's lunch. When the storm had passed, and before abandoning the shelter, as payment for the food they deposited in the pail two nickels and a pair of 16-gauge shotgun shells—he even remembered they were red paper ones with cardboard discs sealing the ends of their waxy tubes and the number 6 printed on both of them. This was in the 1940s, war years, when both money and ammunition were in short supply. "It seemed a fair trade at the time," Dad said.

August in Kentucky is quite hot, with the average temperature at noon often hovering in the upper eighties, or even in the low nineties, so after lunch we always dozed some in the shade to gather enough energy to hunt during the cooler evening hours. We just closed our eyes, probably for no more than twenty minutes, since time on this beloved trip was far too precious to waste on sleep. When we awoke, we stumbled to our feet and looked into the woods, as if we needed to make certain we had not been transported to some other place as we slept, and then we went down to the house in hopes of finding Sherm and Stony at home.

I can see the Morgan brothers now. They are remembered in my mind just as I see them in the only photograph I ever took of them together—a black-and-white picture I made when Gerald Ford was in the White House. I know this because I used the tax rebate issued during his administration to buy the 35 mm camera I used to make that picture. If Sherm and Stony could sit together today, allowing me to make another photograph, smoking and laughing and saying how good they had it while sitting on their porch out in the country they loved, the pose would be unchanged. It was how they always sat out on that porch: a cigarette in their hand, legs crossed, wide-brimmed hats removed, sunburn lines visible on their foreheads and below the hems of their dark shirt sleeves and around their collars, big smiles on their kind and stoic faces, and Old Jack—"Old" was actually part of his name—their faithful, one-eyed cur dog, "our groundhog warrior," as Stony called him, asleep at their feet, the scars from past battles clearly etched on his graying muzzle.

When Sherm and Stony spoke you could hear the soil in their voices, and sometimes in their enthusiasm they would talk almost simultaneously, their words spilling out so close together they almost toppled onto each other.

"We're twins, you know," Stony once told me, "except Sherm's a might taller than me."

"How'd you get the name Stony?" I asked during one of those front-porch sessions.

"Real name's Stonewall," he said. "Our mother's family favored the South during the War and so she named me after Stonewall Jackson. When I was older, she told me that during the War all the grandmothers knitted socks for General Jackson, him being the South's favorite general and all, and that they only knitted scarves and gloves for Morgan and Stuart. She said socks were more important, seein' how an army moves on its feet."

"And how'd you get your name, Sherm?"

"Same as Stonewall," he said. "Only it was our daddy who named me. His kin leaned toward the North and so he named me Sherman after that other general. Don't know any stories about sock knittin' or anything like that, though. General Sherman just marched on army socks, I suppose."

"Belden County was split pretty near down the middle during the War, accordin' to the old folks around these parts,"

Stony said. "Kentucky was what they called a border state, with some folks fightin' for the North and other folks for the South."

Sherm added his two cents to the history lesson.

"We were born in 1895 out in that old house under the hill," Sherm said. "When we was just kids, there was an old man that lived down the road, name of Coedale Spriggs, and he fought in the War for the North. He told us how some families, like his, had brothers and fathers fightin' on opposite sides. Whole damn families couldn't agree on what the fightin' was for. He said he was layin' in the woods, settin' up an ambush one day, when the man next to him told him how he'd killed his own brother two weeks before in a fight. He didn't know it was him till he walked up on him after the skirmish and found him lyin' facedown in the mud. Ain't that the damndest thing to have to live with your whole life." Both Sherm and Stony shook their heads at the thought, both of them understanding how it must be to know you killed your own brother in a war you did not understand.

"I heard a college teacher on the radio last week say that down South they call the Civil War the 'late great unpleasantness,'" Stony said. "That seems a right good name for it now, don't it?"

"Ain't it the truth," Sherm added. "Ain't it the truth."

Looking at their faces, framed in the uneven shadows that were cast beneath those wide-brimmed hats they favored, you could see how the weather and the hard work had sculpted them. They were men of the earth, simple Kentucky hill farmers with an honest kindness that bordered on elegance. They grew tobacco and vegetables and knew the importance of laughing and of sipping a cold beer when the sun was high enough to chase Old Jack into the cool darkness of the dirt beneath their front porch.

These two kind old gentlemen and their ancient farmhouse, an interesting combination of white painted boards and brick chimneys that had been added over the years, are part of my earliest memories of the country, of going "back up home" with my father to hunt squirrels in August, to inspect the tobacco crop, and to sit in the shade of their tin-roofed front porch listening to stories from long ago, some from the day before, and some, no doubt, invented on the day of their first telling for the benefit of my young ears.

One of my favorite stories underscores the importance of politics to the people of Belden County, who are famous for their commitment to the Republican Party. This particular story was about the Morgan boys' pet rooster, named Bruce, whose constant proximity to the brothers was as well-known as their love of a good laugh or an offer to provide a supper of stewed tomatoes and fried bacon, maybe with a cold beer to wash it all down, after a long, hot day of helping them work their tobacco fields.

"When you talked to old Bruce," Stony told me, "he'd rare back and crow. Didn't much matter what you'd said, he'd just crow at most anything."

On the day this particular story about Bruce was hatched, the rooster's absence was obvious to a fellow farmer paying a visit to the Morgan place. This was just after John Kennedy had won the presidency. When this visitor inquired about the rooster, or more specifically about its absence, Sherm and Stony, rather than just admitting it had died of natural causes, are reported to have said that it was a sad day indeed. They feared they had to report that upon learning the Democrats had laid claim to the White House, old Bruce had been so despondent he committed suicide.

Sherm was a tall man who loved a good laugh and a cold beer, and you were aware when telling him a story that he was really listening to you, cocking his head to one side or the other so as to take the words straight in through one ear, concentrating on what you had to say and interested in what you might bring forth. When he stood on the front porch of the house and stretched and looked out over the farm, he went to a place very much inside himself. The land had such a great hold on him—deep in his bones, to the marrow. To my knowledge, he never ventured more than fifty miles from where he was born and raised, and eventually put to rest, nor did he ever seem to want to. The look and the feel of the land around him seemed more than enough for him.

Sherm died some time ago, in a cold month. I remember the roads were icy and snow-covered and I could not travel on the back roads to attend the funeral in Persimmon Gap. I remember how bad I felt that I had not been able to tell Stony and the others who had gathered to show their respect for Sherm just how much he had meant to me, and how I had carried the sound of his honest laugh in my ears my whole life, even remembering it as a connection to home when in 1969 I traveled across the Atlantic for military service in West Berlin.

Except for his army days, Stony never ventured far from the hills where he, too, had been born and raised and eventually would be put to rest beside his twin brother, in the ancient cemetery near the ground they both cultivated, loved, and nurtured year after year. I knew that Stony had served in the army in Berlin at the end of World War II, and so I sent him some photographs I had taken while on a trip to the Berlin Zoo.

"There wasn't any zoo when I got there," Stony told me some years later. "Everything was flattened and blown up. The zoo animals were walking around in the streets. Piles of rubble everywhere. It was an awful damn mess."

A soft-spoken man, his voice so quiet and gentle you had to listen carefully to hear every word, Stony was kind and honest and always seemed at peace with his world, regardless of any rough spots life may have asked him to travel over the years. And I suspect those were few.

5

PERSIMMON GAP

Close to these woods was the little town of Persimmon Gap, the home of the "Undefeated Persimmon Gap Bobcats," the baseball team the town loved, and the beloved place where my father had spent his youth. Like most small Kentucky towns in the early 1960s, Persimmon Gap was quiet and without much commotion except for Sunday services at the Persimmon Gap Christian Church next door to the house where my grandmother used to live. There was, now and again, I suppose, the odd front-porch disagreement on a hot Saturday night, but what went on there was mostly just life, mild and calm.

On the days we did not stay out in Cogan's Woods for lunch, we drove the short distance into town. This was truly a spot you missed if you blinked when driving through on the main highway. Persimmon Gap was a place where scaly water maples lined the main road, their trunks whitewashed and looking like white socks on a black cat. The ladies in Persimmon Gap gardened while wearing brightly colored cotton dresses and straw hats with green plastic visors embedded in the brims. On warm August afternoons there was the sound of rakes scratching at grass clippings on stone paths and children laughing and shouting in the distance. The smoky scent of burning yard waste hung in the air as residents tended to their gardens. The old men, now relieved of the hard, hot work that comes with a life spent wrestling a living from the soil, sat around on the wooden benches in front of the store and whittled and smoked and chewed tobacco, all the while spinning tales and napping in the shade of the porch when the sun was high and the air was still and hot. It was a place where biscuits, country ham, cornbread, and fried chicken seemed to be a part of every meal, and where in the center of every kitchen table sat sweating glass pitchers of lemonade and sweet tea, encircled by glass tumblers turned upside down, awaiting a bunch of thirsty kids and a tired, parched farmer. It was a place where friendly folks wearing genuine smiles offered a kind word and a cold drink on a hot day. And it was where I once went to spend a piece of each summer to be with my grandmother, and where the memory of the grandfather I never knew lived on. It was home to me, the town and my grandmother's white frame house up on the hill, with its squeaky front-porch swing and whitewashed trees.

The Persimmon Gap General Store sat far enough back from the two-lane blacktop that ran through the middle of town so as to allow a pickup truck to squeeze in tight to its twin gas pumps. Between those pumps and the paired front doors, both fitted with sagging screens and blue metal push bars painted in red-and-white lettering with the slogan "RAINBO is good BREAD," there was a long wooden bench that served as a pulpit for the old men gathered there. No doubt some of those old-timers had carved their initials in those benches when they were young, because there were names accompanied by dates as far back as the late 1800s. The men whittled and spat between their sermons and tugged at the bills of their denim work caps to shield their eyes from the advancing sun. Every last one of them had a pocketknife and a railroader's pocket watch, and each was always looking for any reason to show either or both to a nosy kid. Once I asked a favorite old man—Uncle Bill was the only name I ever knew him by—if he had his knife. He nudged his cap bill up with his thumb, looked straight at me, spat in a red coffee can, and said, "I got my pants on, don't I?" I never asked him again.

By the time we arrived in town, it was usually hot enough to soften the asphalt on the shoulder of the road as we stepped past the pumps and joined the old-timers in the shade beneath the porch. We stomped the dust from our boots on an asphalt apron paved with hundreds of flattened bottle caps. There were caps from every soft-drink maker—Pepsi, Tom Collins, Coca-Cola, Upper Ten, Nehi, 7-Up, and others—but it was plain that Persimmon Gap's favorite drink was Dr. Pepper. No contest.

Two steps up and we entered the store, the screen door slapping shut behind us. It was cool in there, the blades of the cranky ceiling fan twirling and murmuring up in the high ceiling. Before this building became a shelter for groceries and hard-working people taking a break from the weather and the toil of farming, it had been a shelter for the souls of the congregation of the now-vacant Persimmon Gap Methodist Church. And now, where the pulpit had been, there was Frazie Brell, the owner of the store, hailing us from her post at the front counter—"my crow's nest" she called it—just behind the big red Coca-Cola cooler inscribed with the message to patrons: "SERVE YOURSELF. DRINK COCA-COLA. PAY THE CLERK."

"Welcome home, George Elbert," she would cackle in a voice that was thin and feisty like her body. "Your mother was up last week. Over to the cemetery looking after your dad's grave. She don't age, George Elbert. It ain't right, you know."

The store was the gathering place for the town, young and old alike. Bare wooden floors, patched in at least a hundred places with tin-can lids, supported old couches, the stuffing falling out of them onto the floorboards, and a half-dozen straight-backed wooden chairs encircling a potbellied stove. Old-timers of various shapes and sizes leaned into their stories from these perches, with one old fellow always seated on a three-legged chair supported by a stack of wooden Coke cases where the amputated leg had been. Truth and lies were to be heard everywhere. It was up to the listener to decide which were fact or fiction.

"He's growed a bit, George," this old fellow in denim bib overalls said, pointing at me. "Soon you'll need to put a big rock on his head to keep him down." He laughed and rocked, his right leg crossed over his left knee, with his white sock folded down over the top of his work boot. He slapped at a fly with his old railroader's cap, one of those high-crowned hats made of what looked like blue-and-gray mattress ticking.

"You missed the big show this morning," the old man said. "A fellow from up in the next county come in here with a red fox stone dead. Real proud of it, too, he was." He spat a long stream of tobacco juice into a red coffee can on the floor next to him.

"To hell, you say," Dad said.

"No, sir. Said he'd shot it right in the face while he was squirrel huntin' in those big beech woods up above the river, below the Morgan place as near as I can figure. We took it away from him, of course. Told him how we'd put those foxes in this country with our own money so we could run 'em with our dogs, not shoot the sons-a-bitches." He spat into the can again. "He said he would be back with the sheriff to get his fox. First off, I told him it wasn't his damn fox, and then I told him how that wouldn't be all that smart, since the sheriff was the president of the Belden County Fox Hunters Club. He wasn't so mouthy after that. And then we run him off altogether."

While Dad busied himself with the business of catching up on the hometown news with old schoolmates and family friends, I scouted for treasures. There was far more interesting terrain for a kid to explore within that single large room, with new items to be discovered every year.

The big, red Coca-Cola cooler was always the first stop for me. I approached it with reverence, lifted the front half of the heavy piano-hinged lid, smelled the icy water, and surveyed the caps of all those soft drinks submerged down in there. There was a flotilla of sodas in different-colored glass bottles cooling down in that watery darkness, their tops just barely above the waterline. I rolled up my sleeve and plunged my hand down, submerging my arm to the elbow. I let my arm soak in there for a time, because the cold water felt good on my hot skin, before plucking out a drink, usually a Dr. Pepper, but sometimes a Pepsi, or "Pepsa-Cola" as the people in Persimmon Gap pronounced it. I wedged the bottle's cap under the opener built into the front of the cooler and snapped it downward, catching the cap in my hand so that I could add it to the blacktop in front of the store on my way out. I shucked the icy water from the bottle, toweled it off against my shirt, and tipped it straight up. With the bottle pointed toward the ceiling, with the dark nectar ran straight down my throat, burning the whole way as I pulled on it for a long, slow drink. After that first satisfying gulp, I dumped in a bag of salted peanuts, shook it up to mix the salt around, and then began my tour of the store.

The penny candy bins were stacked full in the glass enclosures of a massive oak display case. There were Mary Janes, jawbreakers, caramels, bubblegum, Squirrel Nut Chews, and Tootsie Rolls, to name a few of my favorites. I always lingered there, sucking on the cold drink while trying to make a decision about the candy. So many choices, but I usually went for the Mary Janes and the Squirrel Nut Chews.

Between the candy and the back wall was a white metal vegetable cooler. Bushel baskets of fresh-picked corn, tomatoes, potatoes, and other produce were stored there. At the far end of the cooler was a white-enameled pail with a blue rim filled with cool well water, a matching enamel dipper hanging next to it on a nail. This was the community water cooler, before people worried too much about drinking after one another from the same cup. The water had been pulled up from deep within the store's cistern, which was capped with a galvanized-metal hand pump bolted to a large, flat rock above the watery cavern, located outside the back door. Frazie said she tied a piece of clean white rag over its spout every Monday to help filter the water that was brought to the pail.

"There's some strange-lookin' things in that rag every Monday, let me tell you," she said. "God only knows what's down there, and I'd just as soon He keep it to himself."

On the back wall, there were floor-to-ceiling wooden shelves painted the same light green as the walls. This was one of my favorite places in the entire store, because this was where the shotgun shells were stored—box after box of them, from the plain designs of many manufacturers to that of my favorite, the artwork on the boxes of the Peters Cartridge Division of Remington Arms. On the front of each blue box was a greenhead mallard emerging from a swampy piece of ground rimmed by cattails and heading for a stand of trees visible on the far horizon. "Peters HIGH VELOCITY *Rustless* LONG RANGE, HARD HITTING, SMOKELESS SHOTGUN SHELLS," the company proclaimed on the box in bold printing. To a believer, these words were as powerful as the intoxicating smell of spent powder mixed with Hoppes No. 9. I believed because Dad believed in the power of those shells and because I had killed a number of squirrels using those "good-luck" blue shells Dad had given me. I always grabbed a box of 16-gauge number 5 shot from the shelf, which, judging from the number of boxes that were stocked, seemed to be Persimmon Gap's favorite. I opened it carefully so as not to damage the cardboard flaps and stood there in the back of the store studying the contents: the waxy blue hulls glistened under the ceiling lights and were perfectly aligned, their star-crimped ends and shiny brass bases alternated to make room for twenty-five perfect paper cylinders. "PETERS PACKS THE POWER," the company's slogan declared as I closed the lid. I knew the value of loading with those "TRUE BLUES." You could count me among the faithful.

Lunch at the store consisted of a thick slab of baloney and Colby cheese sandwiched between two slices of soft, white Rainbo bread slathered with yellow mustard. A bag of potato chips, a Snickers bar, and a Pepsi or a Dr. Pepper topped it off for me. Dad ate the same, except he favored an Upper 10 or a 7-Up. Sometimes I went outside and sat in the shade on the cool concrete steps and ate my lunch. I would listen to the old men talk and smell the gas fumes as the farmers came in from the fields to fill their trucks from the pumps out front. Those were real gas pumps, painted bright red and equipped with clear glass bubbles on their sides where tiny pinwheels swirled round and round as the orange nectar poured through the hoses and into the tanks of those old, rusted pickups.

The gravel in the road in front of the store popped under the tires as the trucks pulled away and carried the farmers back out to their fields. The sound of the gravel reminded me of the time I attempted to walk barefoot with my grandmother to a friend's house just a short piece down the road. Those rock chunks tore into the bottoms of my city boy's feet as I made it a hundred yards or less that day. No way could I walk barefoot to his house, as my friend always did when coming to my grandmother's to play. I went back to the house for shoes, slowly, and never tried such a fool thing again.

After lunch in town, we always stopped to see Tonk Montgomery, the best squirrel hunter and trapper in all of Belden County. He lived in a big green house that was set into a grove of old dogwood trees on a flat above the railroad. Once when we were visiting with Mr. Montgomery, he told us how he had not had good luck in finding squirrels the previous season.

"There weren't many last year," Tonk said. "I was findin' a few early. They were cuttin' akerns in those big oaks above the church at the other end of town." He spat a long string of auburn-colored tobacco juice into a white porcelain pail sitting on the floor to the left of his chair.

"How many did you kill, Mr. Montgomery?" I asked. I always called adults by the their formal name, until told to do otherwise.

He spat again before answering me. "First off, you can call me Tonk, 'cause Mr. Montgomery is my father and he's long since dead. So call me Tonk, son, long as your dad don't care." He looked at Dad and their eyes agreed. With that settled, he went on to tell more about the squirrels.

"I reckon last year I got a few more than fifty, mostly grays," he said. "Maybe a few more than that." I was certain my eyes had to be bugging out of my head at that figure. I had never seen that many live squirrels in one season, much less that many dead ones. "The season's still young, though," he said. "I might find a few more than that this year before it's all over."

Years later, on a hunt by myself in Cogan's Woods, I would find just after Tonk's death his old rusty traps stored in the crevice of a lightning-carved beech tree that seemed to grow out of solid rock at the edge of a high ridge. Tonk (I had started calling him by his first name shortly before his death, hard as it was for me to do) had wedged a piece of tree bark in front of his stash to help camouflage it from the view of any-one who might stumble onto his hiding place. The tree arched out over the stony edge of the ridge and was far enough away from the main trail that you needed a reason to go over there. Even at that, you had to go up and stand real close to the old beech to see that the bark was not an original part of the tree, that it had been stripped from another beech and placed care-fully within the cavern. But there for searching eyes to discover was a tag of burlap, fluttering in the day's wispy air.

Behind that shield of bark, I found his traps and an even greater treasure—his handmade map of Cogan's Woods. Drawn on a brown paper bag that had been cut apart and flat-tened, the rough drawing contained his name and some dark-ened and blurred pencil Xs that marked special places that held mystery for him and the locations where he preferred to place his traps. He had scrawled a few lines of description here and there, and some of the places that he treasured I knew well. I knew, too, that these same places had produced a sense of wonder and enchantment in me. It was comforting to know that he found solace there, too; I felt an even larger, more important part of his world than ever before. I kept the map and one of those traps, an "ONEIDA VICTOR," the "number 1" stamped out above the trademark "V" in the pan, and put the rest back into the charred heart of the tree, tucking away that flagging burlap tag to keep the secret safe.

Standing there on that day of discovery, I thought back about Dad and how we had hunted past this tree so many times and how Stony had told me that "Tonk Montgomery knows every tree in those woods. Like being in his house, you know, 'cause he spends so much time out there."

I wondered if even then he was using that old tree to store his traps, and if at that time he was drawing up the map, which carried no visible date, adding to it his references to the hollows and glens and the out-of-the-way places in those woods that made him happiest and filled him with wonder.

I remembered, too, another chance encounter with Tonk on that same ridge a year earlier when Dad and I were hunting back to the Mercury. Dad was hunting a lower-woods trail and we planned to meet at the car for lunch. As I made my way along the long-abandoned wagon road, I saw Tonk standing in a clearing among the trees. He was leaning on the only gun he ever used, a long-barreled L. C. Smith 16-gauge double, its receiver already silvered by then, and he had three squirrels hanging from his belt on a brass pin like mine. He recognized me and motioned for me to come over to where he was standing, the big smile on his weathered face shaded by the brim of his faded brown felt hat.

I went as silently as I could, trying to move with the stealth of an Indian, to feel the earth through the thick soles of my boots so as to avoid cracking a single twig. After all, I was being invited by the squirrel-hunting legend of Belden County to join him. I made as quiet a stalk as I ever had in my life, taking my time and choosing with care each step, every piece of ground where I placed my feet. And Tonk Montgomery knew it, too. I could see it in his smile.

I walked up to his right side and whispered my hello.

He placed his unshaven face close to mine. The whiskers were mostly gray, and there was the unmistakable odor of coffee and tobacco as he whispered, "There's seven grays in this pignut to my left. They seen me comin', but I was too close for them to run. They're all hid up there. Ain't none of them left the tree." He spat off to his left and looked back my way. "How about helpin' me kill 'em?"

I couldn't believe my ears. Tonk Montgomery was asking me to help him kill squirrels. It appeared that Tonk Montgomery was not only an accomplished legend, he was a generous one as well.

"You sure?" I asked.

He nodded, spat again, and motioned for me to stand still. Again he whispered.

"I'll circle that pignut," he said. "When I do, they'll start movin' around up there. You stay still and you'll get some shooting. You ought to be in range from here with that four-ten."

Tonk Montgomery pulled the old double barrel up and checked the safety, then cradled it in the crook of his left arm, holding it tenderly, making sure its barrels cleared the spindly limbs of the saplings closest to him as he began his stalk.

I stood perfectly still and waited for him to make his circle. Halfway around the tree on his first pass, a squirrel flushed out of the canopy and ran around to my side. He was up high and fully exposed. I held tight on him and squeezed the trigger. The big gray squirrel dropped straight down. I looked at the squirrel lying dead in the leaves and then at Tonk Montgomery. He smiled and continued to walk around the tree.

Before the circle was closed, I had killed four of the seven squirrels with four shells, and Tonk Montgomery shot the other three, with two shells.

"I've never seen anybody shoot two squirrels with one shot," I said.

"Me neither," Tonk said with a big smile. "It ain't often a man catches two of them talking like that, so close and all."

He cradled the 16-gauge in the crook of his left arm and sniffed at one of his empty hulls before pocketing it—I noticed it was a blue paper shell, like those Peters number 5 shot stocked at the Persimmon Gap General Store. Then he spat in the leaves to his right side and said he would "just slip on out" the same way I had come into the woods. I thanked him again and watched him go, his steps silent and cautious, his eyes taking in everything as he went. He vanished among the trees, like fog mingling with drifting smoke, with a limit of gray squirrels hanging from his belt.

We said good-bye to Tonk Montgomery and went back through town on the lower road, which ran between the railroad and the river. There were a few wooden buildings from before the turn of the century still standing down on the riverbank, with their siding a weathered-gray and every window knocked out. One of those was the town's first post office where my grandmother had been postmistress for many years. It was two stories high with a porch that ran all the way across the front, and it had long, shuttered windows and a pair of padlocked front doors. There was an identical pair of doors nailed shut with boards above the porch roof where a balcony had once been. We rolled to a stop this side of the railroad crossing and waited for an eastbound train to pass through Persimmon Gap. Dad turned down the radio, as he always did at crossings, and sat with his arm sticking out the window. He smoked another cigarette as we watched the boxcars roll by. In a few minutes, two men in bibbed overalls waved with their denim caps from the back of the red caboose. We crossed the tracks and pulled up in front of a vacant field, and Dad shut off the engine. I rolled down my window to listen. The train's eastward rumblings were reduced to a fading click-clack on the rails. Finally, there was nothing but quiet—that and the smell of the river.

Out in the lot, behind a faded, hand-painted sign that declared this to be "Persimmon Gap Field—Home of the Bobcats," we could see the remains of the old ball diamond. It was overgrown now, but if you squinted, you could see traces of the base paths and a slight bulge in the center of it all where the pitcher's mound had been. There were stumps on both sides sticking up out of the weeds, the only remnants of the team benches, and the backstop was a tangle of rusted wire dangling from four vine-choked posts.

"Your great-uncle Thomas threw a no-hitter from out there in 1951, two years after you were born," Dad said. "A lot of people said he was the best pitcher the Bobcats ever had. He was gonna play for the Reds at eighteen, but he cut off a finger on his right hand in a farming accident just before he was to go to spring training. He never considered leaving after that, but he still pitched for the Bobcats and seemed to do all right, even without that finger. Everybody knew he could have made it. Uncle Thomas and baseball meshed real well."

A rainstorm came up from nowhere. The thick drops turned to muddy streaks in the dust on the windshield. I stuck my head out the window and tried to catch rainwater in my mouth. The water peppered my face like BBs and spattered the dust beside the car. The sky was quickly black and a clap of thunder rolled along the river hills. There was some lightning in the distance.

"Better pull your head back in here," Dad said, starting the car. "We'd best get on back out to the woods if we're going to hunt this evening."

As if there was ever any doubt.

6

KEEPSAKE SHELLS

On the way out of Persimmon Gap, Dad always took his spent shotgun shells from his shirt pocket and sniffed at each one before placing them between us on the front seat of the Mercury. He never left any of his hulls in the woods. He picked them all up, out of concern for the woods and so that he could keep certain ones to remind him of special days and moments when life seemed almost perfect. And to make certain he never forgot these events, he wrote notes that contained all the details—like the date, the weather, who he was hunting with, where he was hunting, and why a particular shell was so significant—and then he rolled them into tight little tubes, the diameter of a drinking straw, and slipped them down inside the hulls.

The shells that he keeps he stores in wooden cigar boxes made of wood so thin it reminds me of the wings of balsawood airplanes. The words "Keepsake Shells" are printed in red letters in his own hand on strips of masking tape affixed to the center of their lids. I like to go to the basement and open the big cardboard carton where these boxes containing his mini-memoirs are kept, these notes entombed in red, green, and blue plastic and paper hulls, like miniature time capsules to remind him of days spent in Cogan's Woods. The boxes—there are three of them—are wrapped in the decaying sheepskin-lined leather vest—it is so old and smells so musty—that belonged to my grandfather. He keeps this bundle on top of his father's canvas hunting coat, a faded, threadbare garment that is etched with a mosaic of dark bloodstains across the back of the game bag where he carried his rabbits. "He was a good shot," Dad always said. "He shot a humpbacked Browning 16-gauge. He must have sold it before he died, because I never did find it among the things he left me."

I never knew my grandfather, because he died when I was two years old. But I know how he smelled—like the canvas coat and the sheepskin vest, "genuine, the real thing," as they say. And I know he was a good cook and was said to have made the best biscuits ever. "Light as heavenly air" was how an old man at the Persimmon Gap General Store once described them to me. "Yessir, your granddad could cook," the same old man said. "And he was a good man, son, a real gentleman." I can tell from the way he smelled that it's true.

I like to sit in my great grandmother's walnut rocker with the wide arms, a box of the shells on my lap, and immerse myself in the familiar memories I find there. I want this time to last, so I shut my eyes and reach in and pull out one shell at a time. Very slowly I read the short story each one contains, mouthing every word, as if by doing so I will be able to relive the event and wring the most I can from each short tale penned in red ink in my father's distinctive hand.

In a green paper shell: *August 20, 1966. At old sink hole, on point above the Ohio, killed fox squirrel with this 20 gauge #6 Remington. First time to shoot at anything with new Ithaca 20 gauge. Cutting on Buckeye. Nice cool A.M. By myself. Love the 20 gauge. My mind returned to 1940s.*

In a red paper shell: *August 31, 1963. On ridge above Morgan homeplace, at line fence, by old log operation. I killed first squirrel while using the .410 Winchester Model 42 I purchased from Mr. Mason in Persimmon Gap. This shell, red, paper Super X #5, was included in the deal. Also first kill of any kind with the 42. Ron was along and using the Sears .410. I got 2 and Ron 1. A perfect foggy morning. Working on several hickory along line fence.*

In a blue paper shell: *August 21, 1965. Second squirrel (of 2) killed on ridge at log site using the Winchester Model 42. Ron with me on hunt, he got one. This shell (good old blue) a Peters*

#6, first one used from box purchased on trip to Bald Knob, Arkansas. Young gray leaving hickory, after I had killed one. Lovely morning & a lot of fog.

In another blue paper shell: *August 28, 1965. On a cool August morning using Model 42 .410 killed fox squirrel near Walker's barn. Took 2 shots, final was with this old Peters blue paper #6. Purchased at hardware store going out of business last year.*

In a green paper shell: *August 29, 1964. Made a clean kill with one shot from Model 42 on squirrel in Hickory Nut Grove. Was in crooked trunk hickory (at end of cross path) on Morgan's line. Remington #6, green paper. Wonderful day.*

Again in a blue paper shell: *August 13, 1966. Killed gray cutting in hickory at Morgan's line fence. Late in the* A.M. *.410 Model 42. Peters shell several years old. In* P.M. *on old road at end of Grove Ron got 2 reds in one tree using Sears .410. First time Ron got 2 in one tree.*

In two green paper hulls stuck together: *August 14, 1965. In Hickory Nut Grove, on top of ridge, by path, just in woods, at old barn. Killed fox squirrel traveling just after daybreak. Shell was 20 gauge Remington #6, first one used from new box Ronnie gave me at Christmas. Used second Remington shell to kill gray in clearing. Note: plenty of wild cherries.*

In a blue plastic 20-gauge shell: *August 27, 1966. I killed very red squirrel with my Ithaca 20 on Charlie's old place, where woods jut into open field. In pignut hickory. By myself this* *trip, only kill I made. Purchased this box of Peters 2$^1/_4$-$^7/_8$-#6 at general store in Persimmon Gap. This trip I saw the old crooked hickory that grew out of a tree stump was close to falling.*

In a blue plastic shell: *August 12, 1967. I killed old female fox squirrel on cliffs above old poet's Word Shack. Ron and I also walked the ridge to Morgan's line. What a lot of memory for me on the old ridge. Pat and the pignuts, Denver, Charlie, Don, George, Carlos, etc. This shell from a box of 20s Ron gave me for Christmas. I now have 11 remaining in the box. This fine day, my only squirrel hunt this year. Too late for cutting. Saw Sherm & Stony for a couple of hours. Nice day. I enjoyed.*

And then there is the memory of a day so fine that all of the shells—slender blue paper ones, seven in all—are stored together in a metal Band-Aid can, along with a dried pignut. The note reads:

My Best Day: *August 17, 1968. Hunting alone using my Winchester Model 42 .410 gauge. Peters shells, #6. Large (very tall) pignut tree on fence line near pasture and big oak (takes 4 men to wrap arms around it). 7 shots (waste one) and killed 6 grays (the limit). Left 2 in tree cutting. Walked to the Point above river with empty gun. A Red Letter Day.*

I have read most of these tales many times, but I enjoy reading them again and again. I always find something new to take away with me, some new insight into my father, something about his loves, his passions. During the last reading, I discovered my father's scent encased in one of those boxes, a familiar scent I had come to know after following him through the woods for all of those years: he smells like spent paper shotgun shells and cigar smoke, with the lingering scent of powder and brass and Hoppes No. 9, and a liberal dousing of Old Spice.

He added to these "Keepsake Shells" every year and taught me that the memories one collects on hunts are as important, if not more so, than the game one brings home.

"Try to think about the good times and remember how it felt to be in a special place doing something you love," is what he always said when we returned home after a hunt. "Pulling the trigger is a very small part of being in the outdoors. If you just want to shoot something, stay home and shoot cans off a fence post."

I never stay home. Not if I have a choice.

7

SQUIRREL
TALES

Once, in passing a stand of second-growth woods near the turnoff to the Morgan farm, Dad was reminded of a story about that particular piece of ground, and of a few others. An old man by the name of Clement Ash, who used to live up on Greenbrier Ridge, which lay along the rocky spine above those woods, shot a big fox squirrel out of the top of a gigantic beech tree. The squirrel hit the ground running, and before he could shoot again, it crawled up inside of a hollow tree.

"The old man saw blood on the bark," Dad said, "and decided he would smoke the squirrel out by building a small fire of twigs at the base of the cavity that led into the dead heart of the tree. He got the squirrel out with the smoke and killed it, but not before a wind came up and blew sparks into the nearby woods and set them on fire."

Dad slowed the Mercury and turned onto the gravel lane that led back out to Cogan's Woods.

"You could see fire in the sky up in there all night," Dad said, pointing up toward the woods. "My father was up until noon the next day trying to put it out, along with half of the county. It was one helluva fire.

"Old Man Ash burned up more than 200 acres of prime squirrel woods. Needless to say, he wasn't welcome to hunt anywhere in this country after that. The place he burnt to the ground has been called Ash Flats ever since. That's it right there," he said as we passed the far end of the property.

"Then there was the time my Uncle Kenneth had to work like hell to get a squirrel he shot," Dad said. "That squirrel ran up inside of a hollow tree, too. Uncle Kenneth cut off a long piece of barbed wire from a roll of old fencing lying in the woods nearby and threaded it up inside that hollow tree, twisting it as he went. He wound that barbed wire into the hair of that squirrel and pulled it out of the tree. The big fox squirrel dropped out at the base of the tree and Uncle Kenneth was a bit too quick to grab it. The squirrel wasn't dead and it clamped down hard on his right hand. He had to choke it to death to make it let go of him."

Before we reached the Morgan house, Dad had time for one more story.

"Another time when I was hunting with Uncle Kenneth over there," Dad said, pointing toward the woods behind the Morgan brothers' tobacco patch, "he had another crippled squirrel run up a hollow tree on him. He couldn't get that squirrel out either, so he built a little fort out of green twigs he cut and sharpened and then pushed into the ground at the bottom of the tree. It was early, so we went on and hunted the rest of the morning. When we came back through there after lunch, that squirrel had finally died and let go and dropped down at the base of the tree. Uncle Kenneth picked him up and that was his limit. He could have shot the sixth squirrel of his limit on our way back to check for that treed squirrel, but he passed it up. 'I was countin' the squirrel in the hollow tree in my limit,' he told me. He never shot over his limit, Uncle Kenneth didn't."

There were the legends, too, of how occasionally the squirrels would migrate out of Belden County in years when there was not enough to eat. Thousands of them were reported to have left Kentucky, headed for Ohio by swimming the river. One old man, who the townspeople said was at least a hundred years old, told us one hot afternoon, while sitting in the shade of his porch, "I personally killt a hundred one morning just sittin' in my johnboat a few feet out in the river. They was like drowned rats. They came off the banks in packs. One thing on their mind, I'll tell you. Getting over to Ohio where they could eat. It's somethin' to see. A man ought to see it once in his life."

8

THE
OWL
TREE

O ut at the far edge of the big pasture that butts up against the Morgan homeplace, there is a dead snag of a tree set in tight against the big woods. Its trunk and few remaining limbs, most skinned of any bark, are a smooth, weathered gray, and in the late afternoon, the tree shines like a signal light as you walk past the barn and look out toward the east. You have to know where to look to see it at first, but once you know it's there, you always look for it, first thing. It is a tree that the owls use.

"There's a nice bunch of hickories in along the top of that ridge," Sherm told me one afternoon when we had joined them on the porch after lunch. He stood up from the wooden bench that ran the length of the front window and extended a long, bony finger toward the back of the pasture. "Go in there behind the owl tree. You know where that's at, don't you?" It was the first time I had heard of the owl tree. I wanted to know more.

"Dad knows, don't he?" I said.

"Ought to. He's been walking under it for a long time now. It's close to where the old wagon road runs down over the hill. That owl tree's been there since the Indians come through here, I'd guess."

"I'll ask Dad to show it to me this evening. We're going to hunt out that way."

"Don't let the owls get you. There's a pair that stays out there in those woods. One's a big old bird. We named him Merlin, cause he seemed so magical, the way he came to the house real quiet and all. He still comes up to see us now and again. He's a friendly old fella," Sherm said. He flashed that great smile, the one full of mischief and kindness, and then continued with his story. "There was a fella by the name of Woodrow Twitchell who stayed in the abandoned Methodist Church down in town. He was a poet and a thinker, people said, and he preached some, too, at the Persimmon Gap Christian Church. He used to come up here a good bit. Said he wrote his poems and sermons out in that old shack above our old homeplace. He called it his 'Word Shack.' He'd do just that, you know—work on his poems and all—but I think he come up here mostly to drink some beer and pick persimmons in the fall. He liked those persimmons."

"He liked the wine we made from those persimmons even better," Stony added.

"He did, that's true," Sherm said. "But I think he come up here mostly for the beer. Many a evening he rode out of here leanin' a little too much this a-way or that a-way in his saddle. He always come up here on an old draft horse Clyde Evers kept in the pasture down on the creek. This old owl, the one we called Merlin, would come up the hill just ahead of Woodrow."

"Merlin was like Woodrow's scout or messenger, you know," Stony chimed in from the front steps. "We figured they worked as a team, both of them being thinkers and all."

"Woodrow said Merlin had been part of a big bunch of owls," Sherm said.

"A parliament of owls is what he called it," Stony added.

"That's true, he did call it a parliament of owls. He knew his words, being a poet and all. Anyways, Woodrow said the owl got to comin' to meet him every time he come up the hill on his horse. He started to talk to it and sometimes he read poems to it as the horse picked its way up the hill. The owl kinda liked it, he said, and would follow them, stayin' in the trees just off the trail."

"Woodrow said that Merlin liked poems by a fella named Longfella," Stony said. "Truth be known, I think Woodrow liked that Longfella best and so the owl had no say in the matter."

"He stayed out at that old shack under the hill by himself a good bit," Sherm continued. "Said his words got better the longer he stayed and that he was closer to the Lord in that old place. I think it was the beer talking mostly. The Lord ain't got nothin' against beer. Mostly it's them old churchwomen that do. They wouldn't have nothin' against beer neither, if they'd drink a few themselves."

Stony joined in. "Woodrow carved some words on the front door of that shack. They're Latin words, he told us, something about some old poems. You boys can see them for yourselves when you get out there this evening."

Later that afternoon, with the sun at our backs, we advanced on the owl tree, walking out past the first large hickory tree on the line fence close to a big sinkhole. It was hot and still, not a trace of wind moving across the pasture. From his right hip pocket, Dad pulled out one of those olive drab handkerchiefs he favored and stabbed at the sweat on his face and on the back of his neck.

"There's a few empty beer cans in there you can bet," he said, pointing at a deep depression in the pasture. "That's a sinkhole. People up here don't have garbage collection, so that's where they dump a lot of stuff. These sinkholes have always been in this country. Nobody knows why or how. There are stories about them, though. Some people say they are the devil's work, deep caves that lead down to hell. And then some people say they are just low spots in the ground suited for nothing more glorious than storing trash. Mostly the men dump their empty beer cans in them, trying to hide the evidence from their wives."

The owl tree stood guard at the mouth of a dark opening where a trail led into the woods. Truly, there was an ominous quality present, with the woods all shadowy in behind it. When we were close to it, we could easily see the whitewash of owl leavings on the trunk, and beneath its outstretched limbs that looked like a cross, there were the pellets—tight little cylinders of bone and fur and hair that owls are known to deposit after regurgitating their dinner. There was no wind out there. There were no sounds. There was just heavy quiet and a strong sense of caution drifting in the air.

We passed under the limbs of the tree on the path, and the woods immediately closed in around us as we entered the cool darkness. Dad stepped deeper into the woods and I stood there at the edge, lit from behind and thinking about Merlin and that "parliament of owls" Stony told us about. Dad motioned me to follow him in. As I did, I thought I heard wings and felt a rush of movement in the air, but I saw nothing. I looked down at my boots, the trail beneath them worn deep into the earth after years of hunters traveling through there, and as I stepped further in, a shadow dropped, ran out across the forest floor, and disappeared into the big woods beyond. The owl tree was powerful medicine. Everybody knew that.

Shortly after entering those woods, we hit the old logging road. There were ancient wild cherry trees out there, tall and big around, and on the river side of the ridge was the Word Shack where Woodrow Twitchell used to write his poems and sermons for the congregation of the Persimmon Gap Christian Church, and anyone else, I suppose, who would take the time to listen. It was, I had to agree, a very inspirational spot, with a dense, cool canopy of big trees stitched together, a view of the river valley below, and a true sense of real calm tucked in among all that shade.

Those Latin words Stony told us about were still visible on the front door of the shack, surviving the wind and sun and rain of all those years. Carved in its heavy wooden planking, the door barely hanging by just one large rusted hinge, were the words: "ADEO SANCTUM EST VETUS OMNE POEMA —HORACE." I knew enough Latin from school, painfully acquired as it was, to know that these words from the famous Roman poet meant "SO SACRED A THING IS ANY ANCIENT POEM."

Dad came down off the ridge and stood with me and looked at the words. He said when he was a boy he met Woodrow a few times, when the old poet lived close to the cemetery and dug all the graves in Persimmon Gap.

"He wore a frayed overcoat, a long gray one buttoned to the neck even in August, and a black derby hat," Dad said. "He was tall and skinny and had a handlebar moustache and a bushy gray beard. He lived close to the cemetery in a big house that was about to fall down. The church where he'd lived early on had been bought and converted into a store. People said Woodrow lived over there near those graves so he could be close to the ghosts of his family and friends. He must have been in his late eighties when I met him, but he was still digging all the graves around here even then."

We walked up closer to the Word Shack and looked inside through the doorway. It was one room, not much bigger than eight feet by twelve feet, and there were four windows—one cut in each sidewall and a pair flanking the front door. Not a stick of furniture remained, and the walls were unfinished planks of wood. The floors were mostly rotted and swollen from the rain and snow that had leaked in for years through the holes in the roof, which was more daylight than shingle.

"Don't look like much now, does it?" Dad said. "People back then were glad to have some place to get out of the weather, though. Woodrow liked being by himself, so I imagine he loved it up here. I sure wouldn't have wanted to run into him in the woods on some dark morning, though."

He lit a cigarette and told a story about how his father was going down the hill one night in Persimmon Gap to help his mother bring some packages back up to the house that had come in on the late train.

"Dad said as he passed the cemetery that night he heard some low moaning coming from behind one of the closest tombstones, and so he went over to look around. Just inside the fence, he saw Woodrow leaning up against a gravestone,

stone drunk, singing a hymn to his dead sister. Dad said he helped Woodrow out of the cemetery and took him up to his house and put him to bed. Before he could leave, Woodrow told him not to worry as he'd be alright because his family would be up later to look after him.

"Dad said he told him, 'Woodrow, your folks and your sister are dead. There won't be anybody coming up here to look after you later, except maybe me.' Dad said Woodrow didn't say anything at first, then he leaned up on one elbow and muttered, 'I am but a simple dweller in a valley of myth, traveling toward the light,' and then, just before he was about to say something else, Woodrow collapsed into the sheets and began to snore. Dad covered him and went out the front door. The next morning the sheriff called Dad to tell him he'd found the old man dead in his bed when he went up to pay him to dig two more graves."

Dad leaned over and put his cigarette out against a rock and pocketed the butt before continuing the story.

"Dad said he told the sheriff how he had found Woodrow in the cemetery the night before and had left him passed out in his bed. The two of them decided to have the old poet's gravestone engraved with his last words. So Woodrow left the world with these words carved here on the door and those final words of his engraved on his tombstone. I suppose that's enough for a fella who loved words. Seems like it ought to have come to more than that, though."

We backed off from the Word Shack and started up the ridge to reach the main path that led to a good stand of pignut hickories. That's when we saw the owl. He wore a mantle of dusty mottled grays and browns and was perched on the broken stub of a branch jutting out from the side of an old beech tree. In the dim evening light, he was nearly invisible against the faded patina of the tree's bark, huddled there, almost leaning against the tree trunk, watching the woods for opportunities. From his perch he could easily see the shack. It was as if the owl was standing guard over the memories living there, waiting for the world to be right again, with the old poet riding up through the woods on his slow-gaited horse, speaking lines of poetry. I was certain he always stayed close by, caretaking this place, waiting for his old friend to return.

9

Advancing
Shadows

On a wide flat in Cogan's Woods there was a persimmon orchard located above a large cow pasture, close to Woodrow Twitchell's Word Shack. There were more than a hundred trees in there, some taller than fifty feet, which Sherm and Stony cared for and harvested each year. The fruits from these trees were large and fleshy, the size of small squash, and their skins were the color of ripe pumpkins in an October sunset. I liked being in the orchard when the light flattened out and traces of sun slipped in through a crack here and there in the leaves overhead and ran down the side of a few trees, burnishing their bark with threads of gold. It was a place where you could get lost and hide out in the afternoon in the cool shade and walk around beneath the umbrella canopy, all the while smelling the sweet scent of those big pieces of ripening fruit that flavored the breeze in there. The orchard was flanked, too, on the woods' side by a pawpaw patch, which added the smell of bananas to the wind. The ground beneath these big trees was bare because very little sun could get through the high, dense foliage, and the Morgan boys ran their cows in there, which also helped to keep it clean and "well oiled," as Stony called it.

"All those cows roamin' around in there give them trees shots of good stuff, you know," Stony said on more than one occasion. "The Lord's manure spreaders, without all the mechanical problems."

The orchard came up during many of our afternoon porch sessions. One particular story of note concerned the efforts of a traveling lumberman who had a unique use for the wood from those ancient trees.

"This fella come up here a few years back and asked about our persimmon orchard," Sherm said. "Said he wondered if we would want to sell it. The trees, you know. I asked him what he'd use that old possum wood for."

Sherm spat into the yard and then continued.

"Our daddy called it possum wood. He said that nothin' on this earth loved persimmons more than an old possum, except maybe him. Well, this fella said he wanted to 'harvest' the trees."

"That always means cut," Stony said. "We told him that if we cut them down, we'd lose the persimmons and that pretty orchard out there, not to mention the wine we make from 'em. We asked him why he wanted to cut them in the first place."

"Know what he said?" Sherm said. He got real close to Dad's face, and that smile and those eyes were working over-time. "Said he wanted to make golf clubs out of 'em. Said those old persimmon trees make the best golf clubs. Called them drivers, or woods. I told him there wouldn't be no woods if we let ever'body come in and cut them down for makin' silly things like golf clubs."

"And I said if we let him 'harvest' them, there wouldn't be an orchard out there for us to prune, and then pick come October," Stony added.

"He still said he wanted to cut them. Offered us good money for them, too," Sherm said.

"With no more good sense than that, we just run him off the porch and clean off the place," Stony said. "Damn fool ought to know money ain't no match for big trees, especially those old persimmon trees."

After that, Sherm walked to the edge of the wide porch and looked out toward where the persimmon orchard lay in the hard afternoon sunlight. He swept his stained felt hat off his head and wiped the sweat from his forehead with a naked forearm. He held his hat at the edge of the brim, in both hands before him, and said, "There are places here so fine they're sacred to a man who loves 'em, like me and Stony do. That old orchard is like that, you know. And you'd know it's true if ever you stood out there in the fall beneath those big trees and the bright yellow leaves and smelled the wet ground that come up to you in the wind right after a rain."

He pointed across the pasture with his hat in his right hand and continued.

"Our mother used to dry the leaves we'd gather for her from those old persimmon woods and make tea out of 'em. She liked to take a cup out there and sit under the biggest of those trees. It must've been nearly a hundred foot tall. She said she liked to think that Indian women had come there to rest after crossin' the river and gatherin' persimmons and pawpaws to take on to their huntin' camps. We never bothered her much when she went out there. I can still see her sitting back against that tree drinking her tea. She was a sweet soul, our mother. She truly was."

Stony sat down on the edge of the porch and propped his back against a post before removing his hat and laying it next to him on the porch floor.

"Our daddy said he wondered if the Indians kept that orchard. There was always just big trees out there for as long as we could remember, and the old-timers never knew it to be any different either," Stony said. "Some old man by the name of Cogan owned the orchard, and all those woods out there that you boys hunt. That's been a long time back now. Not even our daddy remembered Mr. Cogan. That's how far back it's been. But ever'body in this country calls those Cogan's Woods. They're not on no official map or anything, although we did find a map of our place here at the house after daddy died. It had Cogan's Woods penciled on it, scrawled down in one corner, in our daddy's hand. Those persimmon trees were marked on it, too. But that's all I've ever seen in writing that calls those Cogan's Woods."

Stony rubbed his hands through his sweaty hair, then fished a Lucky Strike from his shirt pocket and lit it. He blew out a big puff of smoke, looked at the cigarette, and went on with his telling of the tale.

"Some of the real old-timers tell stories about Mr. Cogan. They say he went out to that orchard and talked to the spirits of Indians who're buried in those rock mounds scattered out through the trees along that ridge. The stories say he stayed put up here and didn't go into town much. Didn't bother nobody. He was more legend than real, I guess, as best we know anyway."

Sherm leaned forward on the bench, his elbows resting on his knees with his hands folded, and studied the porch floor down between his boots before going on.

"Besides old man Cogan, other people farmed up here when we was kids livin' in the house under the hill. Millard and Abigail Conway owned most of this ground before we did," Sherm said. "Kept to themselves mostly, and so people talked a lot about them behind their backs.

"Millard's granddaddy harvested that persimmon orchard before us. And Millard built that stone wall around it by himself with the help of an old mule he called Homer. We kept Homer after Millard died. He could still pull some and old Bruce the rooster liked to ride around on his back while Homer plowed. Damndest thing you ever seen. That old mule loved that rooster, though."

Then Stony said, "We'd sneak over here to this very house from our homeplace as kids and peek through the windows, hopin' to see Millard and Abigail dancing. We could hear the music coming out of their old Victrola, waltzes mostly as I remember it, driftin' out over the pasture and into the orchard. We'd hear that music and come a runnin'. Abigail sang a lot, too. Our mother said she sung at an opera house in some big city before marrying Millard. We'd hear her just a singin' as she carried lunch out to Millard in the fields on summer afternoons. Real pretty, too, Abigail was."

"And as kind a woman as ever lived in this country," Sherm said. "Truly a fine woman. Hell, it was said she could run a trapline good as the next man. They don't make 'em like Abigail anymore. No, sir, not a one of 'em left in this country, I'd guess."

We always used all the daylight on this trip. Even as the sun slipped lower in the sky and the shadows advanced on the slopes of the river hills, we continued to hunt. If the woods cooled and the ground stayed wet, the late part of the day could be as fine a time to hunt as those hunts taken in the soft gray light of dawn. Along with the declining temperatures, there was a silence, a perfect stillness in the air, a texture that promised a good hunt.

Squirrels, too, ran from the heat of the day and hid in the breezy, leafy green tops of the trees, stretched out on limbs or snugged into the pockets of leaf nests built up high where the branches swayed with the slightest breeze. When the air felt right—it cooled and relaxed with the coming of the night—the squirrels traveled back out to the feeding areas. They fed in some of the same trees they had favored at dawn or traveled back to others closer to their den trees. The woods were busy with all manner of life preparing to settle in for the night. The hawks hugged the edges of the shadows near the pasture and kept watch out over the grass, looking for an easy meal—a mouse maybe too far from cover or a rabbit tucked back under a thick clump of cool yellow grass, thinking it was unseen by any eyes.

We followed a routine on these hunts, with Dad drifting down over the ridge toward the river and me hugging the tree line along the pasture. On one particular evening, out at the end of the grown-up field, there was a deep tractor tire print that had filled up with water in a low, muddy spot in the grassy lane. Around the edge of that puddle was a strange yellow blob, and it moved. I crept closer and found a cluster of yellow butterflies. Their pulsing wings, all moving in unison, were speckled with black. They were staged there in a large mass on that tiny mudflat. I moved closer and finally they flushed. Hundreds of them fluttered up all around me, a drifting cloud of yellow quiet. When they had all gone, I descended the ridge to a good place where I could watch for traveling squirrels. The cows lay in the shade of the woods that lined the pasture above me. They rose by kneeling on their front legs when Sherm called for them from up near the barn. "Come on up here, you big fat girls," he yelled. "Come on home for the night now."

Sitting there, I leaned the .410 against my right shoulder, which placed the rib of the barrel close to my ear. As a gathering evening breeze passed through the posts of the vented rib, I could hear the wind whispering.

I stayed put on the ridge and thought about that wind, where it had come from and where it was going, and watched the woods. Finally, I decided to move down to a favorite piece of land where Dad and I always met before making our way back to the Mercury and calling it a day. I left the woods and walked back along the tractor road that followed the ridge. In a narrow strip of trees between the pasture and the woods, I found a lone squirrel, the biggest fox squirrel I had ever seen. He was cutting nuts high up in the canopy of a massive old hickory, backlit by the even light of the evening sky. The wind was blowing through his wide tail. I was able to sneak in close by moving only when the squirrel was busy with the fetching of a fresh nut. When I was finally close enough to take a shot, I waited for him to return to his favorite position in the top of the tree. When he did, I was standing directly beneath him with the gun at my shoulder. He looked down and saw me and froze with a big green hickory nut clamped tight in his mouth. He was staring straight at me when I shot him in the face. He never fell at the shot, like I expected him to, but continued to stare at me as he rode out the last of his life up there in the top of the tree. Finally, he let go and dropped through the limbs to where I stood, waiting for this to be over. He fell into the woods on the other side of the barbed-wire fence and laid there on his back with the hickory nut still lodged in his teeth.

I met Dad at early twilight and we admired the squirrel as I told the story of its killing. He had killed a big fox squirrel, too, closer to the point where we had arranged to meet. Dad smoked and told his story of the hunt, and then we sat there looking north, across the big river, listening to the building of the night sounds. Out there on that point at the end of each hunt, we talked about many things, some totally unrelated to the hunting, including my first and only chat with Dad about sex. He was hesitant to begin, but once he got started, he was determined to finish.

"I know about it, Dad," I said, interrupting him.

"You do?" he said, surprised.

"Yeah."

"You sure?"

"Yes, I know, Dad," I assured him.

"Promise that if you need to know more about it, if you're not at all sure about something, anything, you'll come ask me."

"I promise, Dad."

Across the river there was a little town situated in the river bottom that had long ago been abandoned. A boat ramp had been built there recently and was illuminated by a single light. We could easily see it burning in the evening air from where we sat, like a bright, hot star against the dark shadows of the green hills. When I promised Dad that I would come to him and ask about anything I did not know about, well, you know, about sex, he seemed relieved. He looked out across the hills and without missing a beat, he blurted out, "That's the old Church Bottoms where that light is over there." The discussion was officially closed; we never mentioned the topic again.

After that, we sat and looked out at the darkness slowly commandeering the daylight as the August day cooled and the advancing night spread layers of fog along the river, covering the edges of the fading light. When we were certain we had absorbed enough of this place, as much as we felt we needed to keep us strong until our next trip upriver, we made our way up the hill toward the Mercury, moving at a steady pace to stay a little ahead of the darkness and of the memories that lived in the deep, soft shadows out there.

10

LINGERING

We traveled uphill from the point on an old path that connected with the spine of the ridge halfway between the hay barn, where we had started the day's hunt, and the Mercury parked at the far end of the pasture. On one particular evening when I was older, we emerged from the woods and stepped into the big pasture. While I stood in the cool shadows at the edge of the tree line and studied the barn, Dad walked out into the middle of the field and looked off at the hills. What stories that old wooden building could tell, I thought. It had given shelter to the Morgan boys and their family, and to the people who had worked this land before them, probably even Mr. Cogan.

Standing there in the twilight, I remembered back a few years when we, too, had taken shelter in that barn on an opening day, when at dawn, just as we arrived, a heavy rainstorm had settled on the land. That morning, the weatherman on the radio said we could expect the rainy conditions to hold. "There's already more than an inch in the rain barrels this morning," he reported. "It's not like we don't need it. The crops can use a good soaking, so let's be thankful we're getting as much as we are."

We sat in the Mercury and listened to the final words of the forecast. The rain ran down the windshield in unbroken sheets and pounded on the roof. Finally, convinced we would have to sit this one out for a while, Dad steered the Mercury toward the woods and drove up close to the barn doors.

"Let's take some coffee and rolls and go sit in the barn and see where this weather is going," Dad said. "We can climb up into the loft and watch the sky to the east and decide when it's right to go out into the woods."

We swung open the barn doors and closed them behind us. Dawn was filtering into the barn through the cracks between the siding as we climbed up the ladder, the rough grain of each wooden step visible to me in the fresh gray light. Once we were both up there, we dragged two bales of hay before the loft's twin doors. We pushed the doors open wide and sat down on the bales next to each other to watch the weather come in. There was the soft rhythm of the rain on the tin roof—as only rain on a tin roof in the country can sound—and the summer scent of hay mixed with thunder and distant flashes of lightning. Above our heads were heavy wooden beams—ancient rock-hard timbers with drawknife marks along their flanks. Dad looked out at the wet gray hills and lit a cigarette with the silver Zippo. He exhaled a stream of smoke and I watched it drift through the wet air, disappearing into a sky of the same color.

"Squirrels seem to know if a rainstorm is going to be an all-day soaker or just something that passes through quickly," Dad said. "If they sense they'll be sopped in for the day, they'll go out into it and begin feeding, if there's not a lot of wind. Otherwise, they just set tight and wait for the skies to clear."

From where we were seated, we could see a line of hickory trees to the east, and it was clear there was no feeding activity out there. In the smaller second-growth trees that grew beneath the heavy canopy of the taller trees, there were dense tangles of wild grape vines and the occasional crown of mistletoe punctuating a treetop. At the far end of the pasture, toward Persimmon Gap, the sky lightened. The last of the dirty-gray clouds bubbled up over the tops of the tallest trees and advanced on the barn like a big fist, preceded by a curtain of dirty yellow water that rained down on the green pastures and the tobacco fields. Off in the distance, there were fading claps of thunder and the faint blue etchings of lightning against a still-darkened sky.

"That last lightning strike looked like an arrowhead, didn't it?" Dad said. "You know, all of my life I looked for an arrowhead in this country." He drew on his cigarette and shifted his position on the hay bale. "You'd think with all the miles I traveled along these ridges and in these valleys, I would have found at least one. But I never have. Not one. Not anything that even looked like an arrowhead."

Dad lit another cigarette and pointed it at an old blue telephone insulator hanging in a maple tree close to the barn. I could see that the wire on which it had once been threaded—now encased by the rough bark of the tree that had grown over it—had finally rusted through, leaving the little glass dome dangling from the trunk of the tree, idle and no longer essential to anyone for any purpose, except for Dad.

"I'll come up here and get that someday," Dad said, pointing toward the insulator with a fresh cup of coffee in his hand. "When Sherm and Stony are planning to leave here, if I know about it, I'll ask if I can have it."

"Why do you want it?" I said.

"I don't know why. It just means something to me because it's always been there. It's been kind of a symbol that I could depend on. I could come through here and look up and see that blue glass and feel a certain comfort. That's all."

Years later, while Sherm and Stony still lived there, I passed by the maple tree on my way to the ridge to hunt grouse in the cedar thickets below the barn. A foot or more of snow lay on the ground that January day. When I passed the tree, I looked up expecting to see the insulator, seeking that sense of comfort it provided and that I had inherited from Dad, and I saw that it was gone. Only the bent, rusted wire remained. I looked around and discovered a perfect hole drilled into the snow at the base of the tree, just beneath where it had hung all those years. I knelt down and looked into the hole, and there, at the very bottom, was the rounded top of that blue glass dome. I dug it out of the snow and wiped it off on the sleeve of my wool shirt. The side of the dome had a hairline crack, but no other damage was visible to me. Inscribed in one side of the insulator were the words: Hemingray N<u>o</u> 9—PATENT May 2, 1893. I dried it a bit more, then wrapped it in my army handkerchief and tucked it into a pocket of my canvas vest. For the rest of that day I would occasionally check to see that it was still there and that the crack in its side had not worsened as I carried it through the woods. At home that night, I gave it to Dad and told him the story of its finding. Years later, when he no longer seemed to have a need for it, he gave it back to me and I placed it on a bookshelf in my room. I liked seeing it there, the little blue dome emitting the familiar comfort that we had come to expect from it all those many years ago in Cogan's Woods.

That same day, when the rain appeared to be lessening and there was patchy fog ladled into the pasture, Dad said, "Let's take a drive out to the end of the lane and check on that grove of hickories over near the cemetery. We'll see if any squirrels are cutting in there yet."

When we left the barn and were walking out toward the Mercury, it was even brighter outside and the rain had become a fine mist, and Dad asked if I wanted to drive. I had never driven before and, truthfully, was surprised to hear him ask. It was the summer before it was legal for me to get behind the wheel, but what self-respecting 1960s American boy would turn down such an offer?

Dad turned the Mercury around in the pasture so that it was centered in the lane that ran the length of the drive back toward the gravel road. He told me to come around to the driver's side, and while I did that, he slid across to the passenger side. I jumped in behind the big steering wheel and pulled the door shut. Dad did his fatherly duty of explaining all of the "must dos" about driving. When he had finished and felt I was suitably prepared, he sat back, put his hands on his knees, looked over at me and said, "Drive on, mister."

I turned the key and heard the big motor start. I put both hands on the steering wheel and kind of got myself focused on all of this driving business. I reached around the steering column with my right hand and pulled the gearshift back and down, centering the arrow on the big "D." The Mercury wanted to leap forward—it pulled and tugged and wanted to be free, it seemed—but before the journey could begin, I had to reach down and release the emergency brake. When I did that there was a good amount of bucking and rumbling, until I took my foot off the brake and slapped it against the accelerator. We were off much faster than Dad had envisioned—faster, I am sure, than any father ever envisioned he would travel when first teaching a son to drive. It scared me, too, and I took my eyes off the road and looked down for the brake. I pulled my foot off the gas and jammed it hard against the pedal. The violence of the stop threw me toward the steering wheel and caused Dad to shove his hand out in front of him to halt the crashing of his head into the dashboard.

"That was a good start," Dad said, "but maybe just a little slower this time."

I did better after that. I was tall enough to see over the wheel and past Mercury, positioned out at the end of the hood. But seeing clearly was not the problem. I was afflicted with a happiness I had never known before: I had the driver's-license disease, the happy malady that strikes every fifteen-year-old boy in America. It consisted of an initial shot of pure adrenaline that caused the heart to race, the pulse to pound, and the foot to grow heavy. The very thought of driving was enough to make you want to read a book, even a manual without pictures, that was not even associated with hunting or fishing. I settled into the proud rhythm of becoming a driver and steered the Mercury on down the road.

At the end of the lane, near the stand of hickories we had come to check on, there was a family cemetery, and a funeral was in progress. As we crept closer, Dad motioned for me to pull over to the side of the road. Scattered among the hickories was a small collection of gravestones—spare, moss-stained tablets laid out close to each other, jutting up from the shadows. Some were perfectly erect, while others were chipped and canted to one side or the other. A crowd was gathered about a tall man in a dark suit who held a Bible before him. His lips moved, but we could not hear his words. At his signal, four men dressed in baggy suits lifted a plain wooden coffin above the stones and advanced toward a mound of freshly dug dirt. They placed the box on two boards that spanned the hole beside the mound, and when each one had a hold on his end of the rope looped around the box, they kicked the boards away and lowered the coffin into the hole.

"This is the Carr family cemetery," Dad said, looking out his window. "You have some family buried in there, too." As we watched the funeral, an old man in dark clothing made his way toward the grave from the back of the crowd. As he did, the small gathering parted to allow him to pass among them.

"The Ragman," Dad whispered. "He sells rags and dishes out of his wagon throughout this country and sings at all the weddings and funerals. His voice is something to behold, too, let me tell you. Be real quiet and listen now."

We rolled down both windows and sat silent and unmoving in the Mercury. The Ragman stood before the grave. He removed his wide-brimmed hat and held it against his stomach. Then he smoothed down his hair, shrugged his shoulders a bit, and set his feet, like a pitcher getting set to throw. He raised his chin and sang a haunting version of "Oh Danny Boy" that filled the woods. I have never heard it sung so beautifully since.

"His favorite," Dad said. "He sang it at my father's funeral, too."

When the Ragman finished singing, he replaced his hat and stepped away from the grave. The preacher reappeared and went on with the sermon. A few people at the back of the cemetery began to leave, and one old man in a raincoat and a felt hat started our way. When he came up to the Mercury, Dad said, "Hello, Will. I haven't seen you for a long time." Dad extended his hand through the window and greeted the man with a handshake.

"What brings you up this way, George Elbert?" Will asked. He tilted his head toward the car and the rain ran down his lumpy felt hat, dripping off its brim onto the ground beside the car. He had ice-blue eyes, a thick silver moustache, and a tobacco chew wedged in his jaw.

"My boy and I are hunting squirrels."

"Not in this rain this morning, you're not." He leaned his head against the roof of the car and spat straight down into the road.

"No, we haven't got out yet today, but we're headed that way. We came down here to check on these hickories and saw the funeral. Who are they burying, Will?"

"Walter Martin from up near Cedar Creek," Will said. "He was a friend of my father's, so I come up from Maysville to pay my respects. Where you from now, now that you're not from here anymore, George?"

"Down near Cincinnati," Dad said. "South of it."

"That'd still be Kentucky," Will said. "I lived down there myself some time back."

"How far back?"

"Thirty years or more."

"It's not the same world now. You wouldn't know it."

"I hear that."

"I see that the Ragman is still singing at all the funerals around here?"

"He does, George."

"I told my son he sang that song at my dad's funeral."

"That's true. I heard him sing it that day in Persimmon Gap. I was working with two other fellas on the roof of the house next to the cemetery when the funeral started. We laid our hammers down out of respect for your father, George. Dewey was a good man."

Will backed away from the Mercury, leaning his arm against the roof, and looked back at the funeral. "There's a cemetery further up in these woods, called Cedar Chapel, where most of my family is burr-ied," Will said, thumping the thick index finger of his right hand against the opened cozy wing. "Old graves, all of 'em. I'd like to be burr-ied up there myself. When it's time, you know. Not before."

The hills in the wet morning light were like lumpy green

mounds, and the air was much cooler and softer than it had been at dawn. A fine mist had settled into the woods, and more of that patchy fog had crept into the cow pastures at that end of the road.

Dad said his good-byes to Will, then told me to turn the car around in the pasture and head back toward the barn. Will tipped the brim of his drooping hat as we passed, and I drove on in the mist, with Mercury out there on the hood pointed toward the rainbow that was arching out over Cogan's Woods.

"Are you coming with me or are you going to stand up there at the barn daydreaming for the rest of the evening?" Dad yelled from the middle of the pasture. "We need to get moving, son, much as I hate to. There are some stops I want to make before heading home."

I pocketed the memories of that rainy wait in the old barn and walked quickly to catch-up with Dad. When I was walking next to him on the tractor road I adjusted the carry of my shotgun so that the barrel was pointed away from Dad. We moved quickly toward the Mercury, which was just a speck of white at the far end of the long pasture. The dark green hills to our right were silhouetted against the evening sky and painted in alternating washes of drifting shadow and fading light.

"Were you standing over there thinking about that rainy day we had to hole up in the barn?" Dad asked.

"How'd you know?" I said.

"You had the look."

"What look?"

"The look that said that old barn is something special to you and that there was something you wanted to remember. That's all. Is that what it was?"

"It was," I said. "It was just exactly that, Dad."

"That's good. That's real good," he said. He smiled and patted me on the back and we walked on toward the car.

When we reached the Mercury, we wiped down the shotguns and put them away in their canvas cases. We separated out the spent shells and put the good ones back in their boxes in tight rows of five, alternating the crimped ends and the brass bases. We stored our vests and finished field dressing the squirrels. We used the rest of the water from the army canteen to rinse our hands and drained the water off the ice in the cooler. We wrapped the skinned carcasses in waxed paper and laid them in the sandwich tray.

"It's better than working," Dad said. "I'd rather be here as anywhere."

"Me, too," I said.

"Let's go up to the house and set with Sherm and Stony a few minutes. I want to stop and see Walker and then visit at the cemetery before heading home."

We buttoned up the Mercury, and Dad drove out through the pasture on the tractor road. I walked along in front of the car and kicked grasshoppers out of the clumps of long, yellow grass that grew in the middle of the road and opened the gaps in the fences and replaced them as the Mercury rolled past, creeping ever closer to the Morgan brothers' house in the distance. Voices on the radio drifted out of the car window, one announcer offering "baby chicks and ever-bearing blackberry bushes." Dad drove with his elbow sticking out the window, and every now and then he flicked an ash from his cigarette into the air, the little neon shower burning up quickly, never hitting the ground. Before we reached the last gap, a tiny owl darted into the pasture from the woods to my right and snatched up a grasshopper I had flushed. The little fellow, almost elfinlike, made a hard right and angled back toward the trees, settling into a tall, shaggy cedar along the fence line. Home with dinner before dark, I thought.

At the far end of the field, I turned and closed the last gap as the Mercury rolled on toward the familiar parking place in front of the house. I joined Dad as he made his way along the stone path that led to the front porch. As we approached, Stony shouted out through the window, "Come in, boys. Come in and sit awhile."

We stepped up onto the porch and dusted the legs and seats of our pants, then stomped our boots before going into the house. Sherm was sitting on the couch next to the black woodstove, their only source of heat, and Stony was rocking across from him in his favorite chair. There was the familiar and oddly out-of-place pink telephone sitting to the left of Stony on a stack of Montgomery Ward catalogs balanced on the sill of the front window. On a nail sticking out of the wall above Sherm's head, the corner of a calendar, which was clearly marked 1949, peeked out from behind a wad of tobacco-market receipts. On the dark walnut table next to Stony's chair were two sepia-colored photographs displayed in oval silver frames. The first one was of their mother, Effy. She was wearing a long dress buttoned to her neck. Her hair was pinned up and pulled back behind her ears, and she was smiling a young woman's smile. She was standing next to a rosebush that climbed to the roof of a house on a latticework trellis that hugged a brick chimney. The second picture was of Effy, too, but in this one she was standing with her husband, Marshall, a tall, angular man with a farmer's physique and a serious look on his lean face. He was wearing heavy khaki work clothes. Tan lines were visible below his shirtsleeves, which were rolled up above his elbows, and he was holding a cigarette in his left hand, while his right was clasped about his wife's waist.

As was often the case, Sherm and Stony were listening to the Cincinnati Reds on an old Admiral radio.

"It seems Cincinnat-a's about got the best of the Cardinals," Stony said. "I really like it when the Reds beat up on those Saint Louie red birds." The broadcast was scratchy but clear enough to hear the announcer confirm that the Reds had indeed won this one. "That's it, boys," Stony said. He turned off the radio and directed his full attention toward us.

"Did you get any more squirrels?" Sherm asked. He lit a fresh cigarette off of the one he had been smoking and tossed the stub into the stove through its open door. I could see that the cigarette butts nearly covered the small mound of unlit coal.

"I got three grays this morning and a fox squirrel tonight down there above Ralph's," Dad said.

"Was he cuttin' in that big hickory down below the sink-hole?" Sherm asked.

"Yessir."

"That's as good a place as any to find one this time of year."

"I like to kill them out of hickories better than anything else."

"Some of them trees is too damn tall to shoot 'em out of the top of, I guess."

"Just about," Dad said.

"You get any, son?" Stony asked. He crossed his leg, leaned forward, and lit a fresh Lucky Strike, the wrinkles in his face illuminated by the brief flame from the kitchen match he struck with a snap of his right thumb.

"Yes, sir," I said. "I got two grays this morning and a big fox squirrel out on the ridge this evening."

"The boy has done almost as good as you the last two times up, ain't he, George?"

"I let him have those, Stony," Dad said. "I passed them up so he could shoot them."

"Didn't want to clean them anyways, did you, George?" Sherm added.

"I drive and pay for the trip so he gets to clean the squirrels—all of them, mine and his!"

We all laughed and the men smoked and Stony poured coffee for Dad and Sherm, and he gave me a cold Coke in a short, light green bottle. There were a few more stories and then Dad said we needed to go. Stony brought out a big basket of fresh-picked tomatoes and some field corn.

"Take these home with you, son," Stony said. "Your mother will find something to do with all this."

"Take 'em all, boys," Sherm said. "We got more out there than we can stand to eat."

We thanked them and said our good-byes for a long time, standing there on the porch as the light outside flattened and turned ever more toward dark. Stony stood to the far side of the porch and looked off at the land as Sherm talked to us.

"I never cared much for stayin' in town," he said. He was looking out at the big pasture, and his old eyes told how much he loved what was before him. "I need to be out here so I can see the trees and hills right from this porch—hell, right from this spot even. It's all I ever really cared for, you know."

"This is where I need to be, too," Stony said. "I don't need nothing more than all of this." He took off his hat and wiped his forehead with the back of his hand, then stood there, seemingly taking in all that country with his eyes and remembering it, each piece of it. It was clearly his solace, this quiet beauty that drove him through long days of backbreaking work. Everything that had been a part of his life seemed to rest there with him, in his tender grip on the brim of his felt hat.

 As we walked out to the car, the lightning bugs drifted up from the grass as darkness settled onto the ridge.

"There's that old owl," Sherm said. "Hear him hollerin' from down in back there?"

"'Who cooks, who cooks for you' is what he says," Stony added.

"Guess we better get on," Dad said. "I wanna stop and see Walker for a minute and go by the cemetery."

"You boys come back anytime now," Stony said. "Don't stay away so long neither." We promised we would come back soon and then slid, unwillingly, into the car and waved our last good-byes.

Dad headed the Mercury out the lane and pointed it in the direction of the narrow two-lane blacktop. Sherm and Stony stood in the yard and waved their hats across their faces in a half-circle before going back toward the house. Dad flashed the taillights as one last good-bye. We crawled past the dairy barn and the tobacco field at the end of their lane and pulled up in front of the house of one of Dad's old friends. Walker was out on the front porch and knew immediately who had come to visit.

"Ho! George Elbert," he yelled. He waved his hat in the air while walking out to greet us. He slapped the cap down onto his head—one of those high-crowned, blue-striped denim railroad affairs—and screwed it down tighter, with one hand on the bill and the other tugging at it against the back of his head.

"Hello, Walker," Dad yelled.

"You been squirrel huntin', I guess," he said.

"This morning and some this evening, all of it out in Cogan's Woods."

"Must-a been you I heard goin' in early this mornin'."

"Could-a been us. We came through just before daylight."

"Thought you might be up, now that the law's come in. Any luck?"

"We did real well. We got a few grays this morning and a fox squirrel a piece this evening. Ronnie got his out on the ridge in those hickories above the old Morgan homeplace, and I got mine in a pignut tree above Ralph's barn. I saw five more grays in that big hickory next to those wild cherry trees that stand close to the old road to town. You know the place?"

"Whereabouts did you say?"

Dad got out of the car and squatted down with his old friend in the dirt next to the Mercury, in a wide beam of dusty yellow light beneath the yard lamp nailed to a big sycamore tree. They drew within that circle of light in the dirt of the road with the points of their pocketknives, shapeless lines in the dust to the uninformed. And then they hunkered down, squatting low to the ground, the seats of their pants nearly touching the tops of their boots, to make sure they both knew where that big hickory was located.

"Up near where the fence crosses above Ralph's sinkhole. Where old Ike McMann had to kill his horse when it went down in a groundhog hole and broke its leg. You remember that place?" Dad said.

"Sure enough. You say there was five in there?" Walker said.

"Yessir."

"Didn't get any of them?"

"Not one. They saw me before I could get close enough to shoot. There were five young gray squirrels in there just cuttin' away. I'm certain."

"I'll get out there tomorrow morning before daylight," Walker said. "I'll pop one or two and get back here for breakfast. They eat good, those young grays, and make tasty gravy, too."

They both laughed. We all went around to the back of the car and Dad opened the trunk. He lifted the cooler lid and took out two cans of Pabst Blue Ribbon and offered one to Walker. He passed me a root beer and we all stood and drank and looked out over the pastures surrounding the barn. A thin line of smoke drifted up from the chimney of the house and hung there in the thick, quiet air. Nobody said anything for a minute or two. Walker broke the silence, asking Dad about his mother.

"How's Helen?" he said. He lit a cigarette and offered one to Dad.

Dad shook out one from his own pack and lit Walker's and then his.

"Mom's fine. She lives down in town now, since Dad died," he said.

"I sure miss seein' your dad," Walker said. "He was a good honest man and a gentleman. He never harmed nobody and I never heard anything against him all his entire life. He was as good a friend as a man could ask for. He come out here real regular like and we'd sit and smoke and talk about huntin' and the old people. Most of them are gone, too, and this country ain't the same without 'em. Don't think there'll be many like them anymore. This land'll probably go to hell without the old ones. The young ones don't give a damn for this land or the old homeplaces where they was raised neither. They want to run to the cities and be all busy much of the time. Damn if I understand it."

Walker tipped his can of beer way back, drained it, and shook the last drops from the can. "You boys best be headin' home," he said, crushing the can and putting it into the pocket of his denim barn jacket. "You got a long drive ahead of you and the night's comin' fast. It's tough enough gettin' out-a here in the daylight. It's worse when the light's low and you can't see the bad places in the road. It's going to be a dark night, too—dark enough to tamp down a lightnin' bug's glow to nearly nothin', as my old granddad Vance Henry used to say."

We said our good-byes and promised Walker, too, that we

would come back soon. The two old friends shook hands and slapped each other on the back. Walker went to the house and Dad slid in behind the steering wheel of the Mercury, started the big engine, and put it in gear. Neither man looked back.

The Mercury jostled us about as it wrestled with the potholes and bumps in the road until it found the familiar feel of the blacktop out on the main highway. Then we rolled on toward Persimmon Gap, with more speed and purpose.

In the quiet interior of the car, I thought about how on this annual trip I always wanted to stay longer among the trees and the people, to hunt the squirrels and breathe the air laced with the smell of just-spent shotgun shells, to unravel the mystery of the vanished spring, and to imagine again and again the taste of those tomato-and-bacon biscuits eaten from a tin lunch pail while hunkered under a lean-to during a summer rainstorm. This trip, these people, all of the imagery around me—all gifts, lasting pictures etched in sunlight that washed down the tree trunks and mixed with the stories that were told with reverence among whispers of wind emerging from the thickets and woods, smelling of cedar and tasting of the hills and water and rock, sun and moon, and those ripening persimmons.

But mostly I just wanted to continue to be with my father when we loved only these woods and these people, when being father and son was all there was, all that was necessary when under the spell of Cogan's Woods.

11

ALL THE WAY TO HEAVEN

The Mercury eased its way along the road and up the long hill that led out of the bottoms and toward Persimmon Gap. A creek twisted through a meadow to our right, and as we gained the top of the ridge, to our left lay a broad valley that stretched toward the Ohio hills. The valley narrowed at its middle and then descended rapidly as it ran toward the horizon. At its north end, it became a wedge of deep green spattered with woods and pasture in a checkerboard pattern along its floor. A clear stream flowed down its middle, looking more like a silver thread by the time it reached the far side, until finally it disappeared, running to meet the river in the distance along the outer edge of Cogan's Woods.

This valley lay across the road from the house where I first met her. She was Muriel Beecham, a girl of sixteen, two years older than me. I was staying in Persimmon Gap with my grandmother that September weekend and we had taken a ride with my great-uncle Thomas to visit with Muriel's grandparents. The adults left us standing across from each other out in the front yard, while they went to visit in the deep shade of the front porch.

She had strawberry blonde hair that blew in loose strands across her face in the breeze. Her face was freckled and her eyes a shade of deep green I still cannot describe. She was tall, taller than me, and she wore a flowered dress the color of the sun. She smiled and asked if I wanted to pick apples. I nodded. I wanted to say more, to say anything, but my throat was so dry and tight.

Hickory trees lined the front yard, and their yellow leaves rattled overhead as we crossed the road and went into the orchard that stood on a bench above the valley. We picked Yellow Transparents and sat together beneath the largest of the trees, in a place where we had a good view of the valley. We ate those apples and looked off into the heat. Muriel did most of the talking, while I listened and stole glances at her freckled face.

"This is our valley," she said. She looked over at me and I looked quickly away, out toward the horizon. "My great-grandpa Beecham says you can see to heaven from right up here. Do you believe that?"

At that moment, I believed it because Muriel said it was so. I took another bite of the apple and wiped the back of my hand across my mouth. And then I looked back at Muriel and her green eyes and strawberry blonde hair, and for the first time in my life I knew that heaven had another side.

"I do," I said. That was all I could muster.

We went back to eating our apples and sat there in the warm grass. I was certain on that day that Cogan's Woods was richer because of Muriel and the memory of her that would linger in the breezes and the light up on that overlook. I was certain, too, that the trees and the pastures and the stream down in that valley would not mind sharing heaven with Muriel.

And so every year after that first meeting, I made it a point to ask Dad to stop there on our way into Persimmon Gap and have a look at the valley. Dad would pull onto the shoulder of the road at the orchard, which was mostly abandoned by then, and we would walk among the apple trees to reach the overlook, taking the same path Muriel and I had on that sweet September afternoon. We always picked a few apples— besides those Yellow Transparents, there were a few trees loaded with sweet speckled Russets and big Wolf Rivers—then we would stand out on the overlook, cutting the bad spots out of the apples with our pocketknives, and watch the valley cool.

On one trip, when I was much older, Dad pushed his hat back on his head, folded his arms across his chest, and stared out toward the river and the hills. The ragged edge of a bruised sky rested on the dusky outline of the hills as a flock of crows crossed in front of the sun, now a perfect disc of warm orange out in the middle of it all. We stood quietly in the heavy scent of apples until Dad broke the silence.

"I always loved this valley," he said. "When I was a kid, I helped my Grandad Carr farm his place near here. Most families had gardens and a few cows, and just about everybody worked some tobacco. Most of us thought we'd be farmers. It was the only choice we had, besides going to work on the river or the railroad. I chose the railroad, like my father. Nobody really wanted to leave here, but we had to find work, and by that time it pretty much meant leaving. It wasn't a bad choice, but I wish I could have stayed."

He cut a piece out of his apple, stuck it on the point of his knife, and pointed at the valley with it.

"Old man Beecham owned this valley, and he always said a man could see all the way to heaven from up here," Dad said. "Do you believe that?"

"I believe it," I said, smiling and remembering.

In the meadow below us, a red fox had been mousing in the heavy yellow grass—arching its back before springing straight up and then pouncing down on all fours with its head directly above the intended target. Three times the fox performed as such, before emerging with a mouse, its hindquarters and tail dangling out the right side of its mouth as it trotted off into the woods with its prize. All that had come from that day rested with us up there and settled into our hearts and minds as experience and memory both.

By the time we started back toward the Mercury, the sun was well west of the overlook and the evening sky was lit by an echo of the former light. Deepening breaths of shadow clung to the sides of the valley as the earth cooled and awaited the luminous chalking of the moon. In that light, we walked side by side, my father's hand resting on my shoulder and my hands shoved down into my pants pockets. There was only the scent of the apples and the sound of our boots on the earth and the whisking of our pants legs in the long grass of the orchard.

12

LEAVING

We went there last, on every trip, to the cemetery, its borders defined by a protective ring of century-old maple trees and a waist-high woven-wire fence, always freshly coated in luminous silver paint and tightly stretched along a line of sturdy, gray, weathered locust posts. Across the road sat the Persimmon Gap Christian Church, where Dad had been baptized by Brother Hollis Conway, his hunting partner who came to Persimmon Gap each August to preach at "the gathering."

When we pulled up in front of the cemetery gate, Dad shut off the engine, lifted his hat, smoothed his hair back, and said, "Hollis dunked me in Blue Creek down there." He pointed to the creek crossing under the road below the church. "It had been raining for two days and Blue Creek was high and muddy the day of the baptism. Hollis enjoyed dunking me in that gunk way too much. Held me under too long, I thought, so I never gave him the first shot on a squirrel after that day."

Brother Conway was often the focus of Dad's stories when we sat in the Mercury and looked out at the cemetery. The closeness to the graves seemed to bring out the remembering in him more than other places we visited.

"Once when he was preaching at the gathering, another preacher told Hollis he thought he should spend more time saving souls and less time hunting squirrels," Dad said. "When Hollis suggested the man should try mixing in some hunting with his own preaching, the fella said he was too busy at the work of saving souls to mess with squirrels.

"Hollis told the man, 'It's true, hunting's not the Lord's work in the truest sense, but never-the-less, brother, never-the-less, we need to renew ourselves if we are to stay strong and help other poor souls. So I hunt to renew mine, brother, I hunt.'"

Dad smiled and lit a cigarette and rolled down his window.

"Just after Hollis said that to that old preacher, the number 92 train came roaring into town," Dad said. "Hollis cut the small talk with the preacher and finished his sermon, because he knew my dad was on that train and that once he got off 92, he'd be headed straight to his favorite woods near here to squirrel hunt. Hollis knew there was one big hickory the squirrels were cutting heavy in those woods and that he would have to run like hell to beat Dad there."

Dad laughed at the memory.

"Did Grandpa get there first?" I asked.

"Barely. They ended up killing a limit of squirrels between them and we had a platter full of fried squirrel with my dad's biscuits and gravy that evening. Nobody was a better country cook than Dad. Nobody—not even Mom."

Often when we arrived at the cemetery, the congregation, or "the flock" as Brother Hollis Conway referred to them, would be gathered in the church, practicing their singing for the Sunday services. It seemed that often they were singing the same hymn when we arrived, rehearsing a verse from an old favorite classic we had heard time and again, as if we were expected and they did not want to disappoint us. Their voices blended as old and young alike belted out the familiar words, "Sweet hour of prayer that calls me from a world of care." And sometimes the church bell would ring, echoing inside of its white clapboard tower as I sat in the car and waited for Dad to make the short walk to his father's grave. Through the Mercury's windshield I could see him standing there above it, focused on his lonely vigil, his green hunting cap held before him, both hands crossed and pulled in tight against his stomach, staring straight down at the grass in front of his boots. Now and again he would raise his head and look back toward the car, or off toward the railroad and the river. With the window wide open and the August night demanding what was left of the light, I could hear tree frogs and crickets and the occasional grinding of truck gears on the highway in the distance, and I could see Dad's lips moving, his head still bowed.

I knew when he stood out there that he was tending to more than the physical grave. He was trying to make something right between him and his father, to close the distance that he often told me had been placed between them by his father's long absences from home as a fireman on the railroad. I knew it was the time and place for that kind of remembering, with the night wind brushing against the earth where others before him had visited with their loved ones, and who now lay in their own graves, waiting for sons and daughters to come and sit with them in the dark, if only for a short while, to talk some with them in whispers as fireflies emerged and danced over the tombstones, their tiny lights winking and disappearing in fading smears of chartreuse light.

After a while, Dad left the graves and passed between the heavy gateposts. He then turned to snap the latch of the metal gate. Back in the car, he put both hands on the steering wheel and stared straight out over the hood and said it was time to go. I could tell from his voice that he had been crying out there in the dark. I sat there in the car and worried about my father's grief, and I wondered, too, what words he had whispered during his lonely vigil. I wanted him to be all right, to not be so troubled after such a great day in Cogan's Woods. I wanted things to be better for him.

Sitting there in the car, Dad pointed to a speck of light shining through the deep woods across the road, in behind the church.

"That's Coffin Hollow up where that light is coming from. They took the wood out of there to make the town's first coffins," Dad said, pointing again toward the light. "Hardly anybody would hunt up in there when I was a kid. The old-timers said it was haunted with the promise of all those dead folks.

"My dad said the man who owned it, old Emmett Wilson, liked for everybody to believe that so they'd stay out of there so he could hunt the squirrels up there all by himself. It was true, Emmett was quiet about his hunting and fishing. I remember once as a kid he brought a big catfish into the store and threw it up on the meat scale. It weighed more than forty pounds. Emmett told everybody he'd hung it on a trotline in the river. A few months later, after downing a few too many beers out of the back of my dad's truck, Emmett told Dad he'd caught that fish with his hands, out of the trunk of a submerged car down in the creek below the cemetery. That's how he was. He knew where every damn creature in this county lived. Old Emmett was something else."

On one trip, as we sat in the Mercury preparing to leave, we heard a bullfrog croak twenty-one consecutive times from a pond in the cemetery. As we listened to this amazing solo, we

watched a pair of rabbits running wildly about the tombstones, acrobatic shadows jumping and cracking their hind
feet, chasing each other as if dancers on a stage. The rabbits
were long and sleek and seemingly unafraid. Even the Mercury's headlights washing across them as Dad blinked them on
and off would not cause them to freeze, or to run from the
graves. Our presence seemed to encourage their appearance
rather than prompt their departure. There was no fear in their
movements. They just danced in the Mercury's headlights
among drooping clumps of grass scattered against the base of
the tombstone. The old man buried beneath their grassy stage,
my grandfather, was known to be a serious rabbit hunter. He
kept black-and-tan beagles and always hunted with that 16-
gauge Browning automatic that had since disappeared. In a
faded black-and-white photograph pasted into the family
album my grandmother keeps on her coffee table, he is wearing a stained canvas hunting coat and matching tattered and
patched brush pants, and he is smiling broadly beneath a dark,
wide-brimmed, felt hat. He is young and tall and looking fit,
and he seems perfectly happy, with the Browning tucked under
his left arm, a pair of beagles sitting to his right, and seven rabbits hanging on a clothesline behind him. Written in white ink
in my grandmother's handwriting at the bottom of the picture
are the words: "A Fine Day for Dewey and His Beloved Dogs."

On one of the last trips we made to the cemetery, the
town blacksmith engaged Dad in conversation as they were

departing that quiet darkness. I knew about this man who not only fashioned things with metal and fire and shoed horses and repaired broken farm equipment, but who at that time also dug the town's graves, by hand—the big man the old people had nicknamed "Bones" Henderson. On this particular night, Bones hailed Dad from the shadows as he walked among the headstones headed for the front gate and the Mercury.

"George Elbert," Bones said in a loud, deep voice, waving a lantern before his shadowed face.

"Bones," Dad said. "How'd you know it was me, in the dark and all?"

"Only one man who comes here in a white Mercury year after year. Nobody else, that's for sure. Nobody else."

They talked in whispers for some time, and then I heard the big man's voice grow louder in the dark.

"I just dug another grave for Sunday burying," he said. "That's another one asleep in Jesus this week. Three since Tuesday. I keep busy, there's so many of 'em these days. The old people are tired and ready now." They were close enough that I could see them silhouetted in the lantern light. They shook hands and Dad patted the big man on the shoulder.

"You take care now, Bones," I heard Dad say. "Say hello to that sweet wife of yours. You got one of the finest women in all of Persimmon Gap when you married Bertha. You truly did. Tell her I'll stop by the house on my next trip up home."

The dome light went on as Dad opened the door and slid in behind the wheel. The old gravedigger shouldered his shovel and held the lantern before him as he walked the path toward the main road. He was walking close to my side of the car as the interior light went out, and as he passed, he held the lantern up to my face, obscuring his. The flame hissed, strong and steady behind the glass globe, and the unmistakable smell of blackened kerosene smoke drifted in the night air outside the open car window. The big man's voice came out quietly this time.

"It's important to remember, son," the old gravedigger told me in a voice slightly above a whisper. "Your daddy knows that more than most. It's best you learn it, too."

He lowered the lantern, climbed down the steep bank, and crossed the grassy drainage ditch to the road. I heard his heavy boot steps in the gravel, then I saw the lantern swinging from side to side as he traveled uphill away from town. I watched him go, until there was only the dim wash of the lantern's light in the blue-black night, and then a final flicker that was swallowed by the dark hills.

That night, before we left, in the light of the Mercury's high beams, we dug up a little cedar tree growing next to the cemetery fence. We wrapped its roots in a wet paper towel, sprinkled them with dirt, and placed the little bundle in a paper cup for the ride home, its sweet Christmas smell filling the inside of the Mercury. Later we planted the tree in our backyard, where we could see it from the patio, and every day we would say how fine it looked and how much bigger it was getting. We looked after the little tree with great care, giving it plenty of water and staking it up as it grew so that it would stand straight and tall.

Years later, sitting in a deer stand on a cold November morning and looking out over a cedar thicket, I would be reminded of that little tree and those days spent in Cogan's Woods with my father as I looked down at my young son sitting next to me, bundled in wool and down, his head resting against my arm so as to sleep some before the dawn brought the excitement of his first deer hunt. And in that remembering, I was moved by a newfound clarity of the grief my father must have labored beneath all those years ago in the Persimmon Gap Cemetery. I wept quietly in the darkness, weeping not just because of this new understanding, but because of the painful images I had now of my own father's imminent death. Only days earlier I had sat on the edge of his sick bed to try and comfort him as he died slowly of cancer. Even in the dark of the bedroom, I could see that his once-heavy frame was painfully diminished, nearly skeletal by comparison to the healthy man I knew and loved. His hair was coming back in after the chemotherapy but was returning as solid gray, while before the treatments it had been thick and completely dark. He was so sick and frail, yet he was able to gather his strength to raise himself on one elbow, extend his other hand to me, and repeat out of the dark in a soft, comforting voice—suddenly I was twelve years old again with him whispering to me as we waited on daybreak in Cogan's Woods—the words of the old gravedigger: "It's important to remember, son. It's so important to remember."

With the Mercury pointed toward home, Dad smoked and sipped his coffee while we talked and I tuned the radio to WLW, listening for baseball scores and, as always, the weather. Off toward the river, the tops of the tallest trees were feathered by the night wind and the fields beside the road were bright with the coming of the moon. In the distance, there were lone farmhouses and barns that looked peaceful in that light, while behind us were the darkened woods and the fresh, new memories that would sustain us until next year. In the car's interior, in a wash of the dashboard's soft blue light, we slowed the beating of our hearts as we rode along in the night, the sky spattered with irregular groupings of stars and the lights of hillside farms stretched out in the dark before us, like luminous strands along the backbones of the distant ridges.